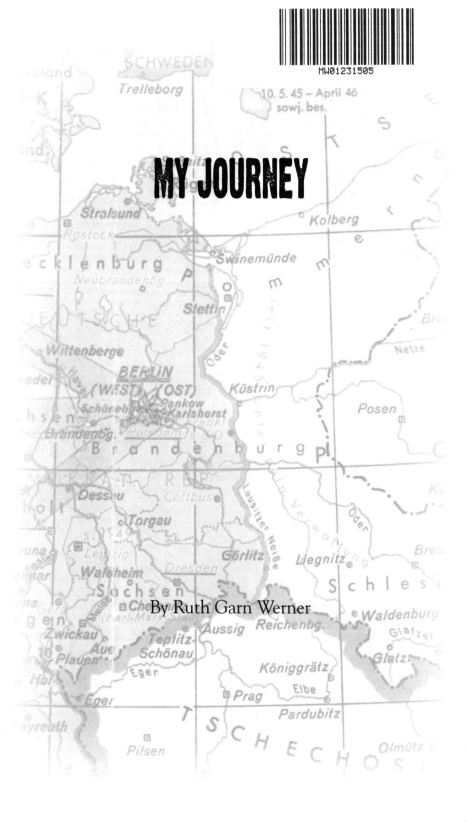

MY JOURNEY

By Ruth Garn Werner

ISBN: 978-1-57579-407-5

Library of Congress Control Number: 2009929418

Printed in the United States of America

PINE HILL PRESS
4000 West 57th Street
Sioux Falls, SD 57106

I dedicate this book to my three daughters,
Edith, Karin and Barbara…

and to my grandchildren and great-grandchildren,
so when they read it and see that life can bring great difficulties
they will, also, see that with love and trust in the Lord
they can and will survive.

Thank God, dear children and grandchildren,
for the life you have been given. Cherish it. Be compassionate with each
other. Always keep in touch with each other…you are family.

To Darlene
God Bless You
Ruth Werner

I wrote this book in honour of my dearest mother,
who kept us alive, kept us safe, kept us moving forward but,
most importantly, kept us together. She showed us
who to look to for help at the worst of times and
who to thank at the best of times…our Heavenly Father.

Thank you, my precious mother, for passing your faith on to me.

A special thank you to my daughter, Edith,
who made this book possible with her endless hours of research,
typing, mailing, emailing, and, it seems like, millions of phone calls.

I hug you, my dear,
your Mama

CONTENTS

PROLOGUE

It was in the year 1927, in the month of April, when a young girl named Ida left her homeland, Germany, and immigrated to Winnipeg, Manitoba, Canada. She was only seventeen years old.

My Mama, Ida, was the youngest of five children belonging to my grandparents, Karl and Alwine Preuss. Hulda, her only sister, was the oldest and then three brothers: Heinrich, Wilhelm and Walter. They lived on a farm located in Klein Gorschen, a village in Kreis[1] Thorn. World War I began in 1914 and Opa (Karl) was drafted to go to the Russian Front.[2] Alwine was left behind to take care of the farm and five children. Ida was 5½ years old when her beloved Mama (Alwine) died. (It's believed she died of cancer.) Opa came home for the funeral but had to return immediately to the Russian Front leaving his five children home alone. The three older children ranged in age from sixteen to eighteen years and they all joined together to get all the work done. Because the family continued to experience extreme hardship they hired a housekeeper who was a friend from the nearby village. When Hulda was nineteen years old, she became very ill with pneumonia. She died and joined her mother in heaven. Opa was called home on emergency leave and arrived just in time to see his daughter buried at the cemetery. After one week he had to leave for the battlefront and the children were, once again, left alone. But this time the situation was even worse. Opa's brother, Onkel Martin, worked many hours at the farm helping with the work and, especially, taking care of little Ida. (Ida has many memories of this time. She, also, remembers how her brother, Heinrich, looked after her and how the farm was being tended to.)

Opa came home at the end of the war and after four and a half years as a widower, he married a woman who was twenty-three years younger. As is so often the case in similar situations, Ida and her brothers found it very difficult to adjust to their new stepmother. Because Ida was a girl, the adjustment was much more difficult. So, in 1927, when an invitation arrived from Ida's aunt to come and live with them in Winnipeg, Manitoba, Canada, Ida decided to go and be with her real mother's sister. Her aunt and uncle agreed to pay her fare if she would come although this was expected to be repaid later. Ida's world suddenly seemed much brighter and she hoped and dreamed about a better future in Canada. Times were so difficult in Germany right now, not only with her stepmother, but also because of the war and its aftermath.

In the spring of 1927 Ida left Germany and went to Winnipeg to live with her aunt. After she had been there for about two weeks, she realized that her aunt had only brought her there in the hopes that she would marry their adopted son. When she discovered that the son had a criminal record she made plans to move from her aunt's home as quickly as she could. Ida was able to get assistance from a local Baptist church. They arranged a room in a boarding house, which she shared with her cousin, Bertha Busch. Ida and Bertha became very good friends. She, also, was friendly with the other young women living in the same boarding house.

Ida went to work in a pickle factory working long hours in order to repay her aunt for her fare. In 1928, the second year of her stay at the boarding house, one of the girls living in the house got married. Unfortunately, Ida had to work late and was unable to attend the ceremony but she *did* get home in time to change clothes and join the wedding reception being held at the house. At this celebration she met the very handsome best man...Johann Garn.

Johann was the youngest child in a family of nine...seven boys and two girls. He was born in Tomaschow, Poland (a small village comprised of German farmers who had settled there) but had immigrated to Germany as a young man. There, he worked in the coal mine near Botrop until he had saved enough funds to enable him to fulfill his lifelong dream of becoming a baker. He served his apprenticeship in Ruhrgebiet in the Rheinland of Germany, specializing in yeast dough. In 1926, unemployment became so severe; he decided to immigrate to Winnipeg, Manitoba. Three of his brothers already resided there and Johann obtained a position at the Canada Bakery. Later he became a partner with Mr. Zanke in owning and operating the National Broadway Bakery in Winnipeg.

After meeting each other at the wedding reception, Ida and Johann dated and fell in love. They were married July 20, 1929. Johann and Ida's first child was born on April 19, 1930. Harry Herbert weighed a scant four pounds. Harry was a colicky, nervous baby who was difficult to care for. When he was nine months old, Ida was shocked and dismayed to learn that she was, once again, pregnant. She had no difficulties during this pregnancy and, as time passed, anticipated the arrival of this child with pleasure. On October 20, 1931 Johann and Ida had their second child, a daughter they named, Ruth. Ruth was a big girl who weighed over ten pounds!! "This baby," Ida said, "was a blessing because she was so good!" And why not? This baby was me!!!

Mama just before she immigrated
to Canada in 1927.

Mama and Papa's wedding day, June
29, 1929 in Winnipeg, Manitoba.

Harry, two years old, in
Winnipeg in 1932.

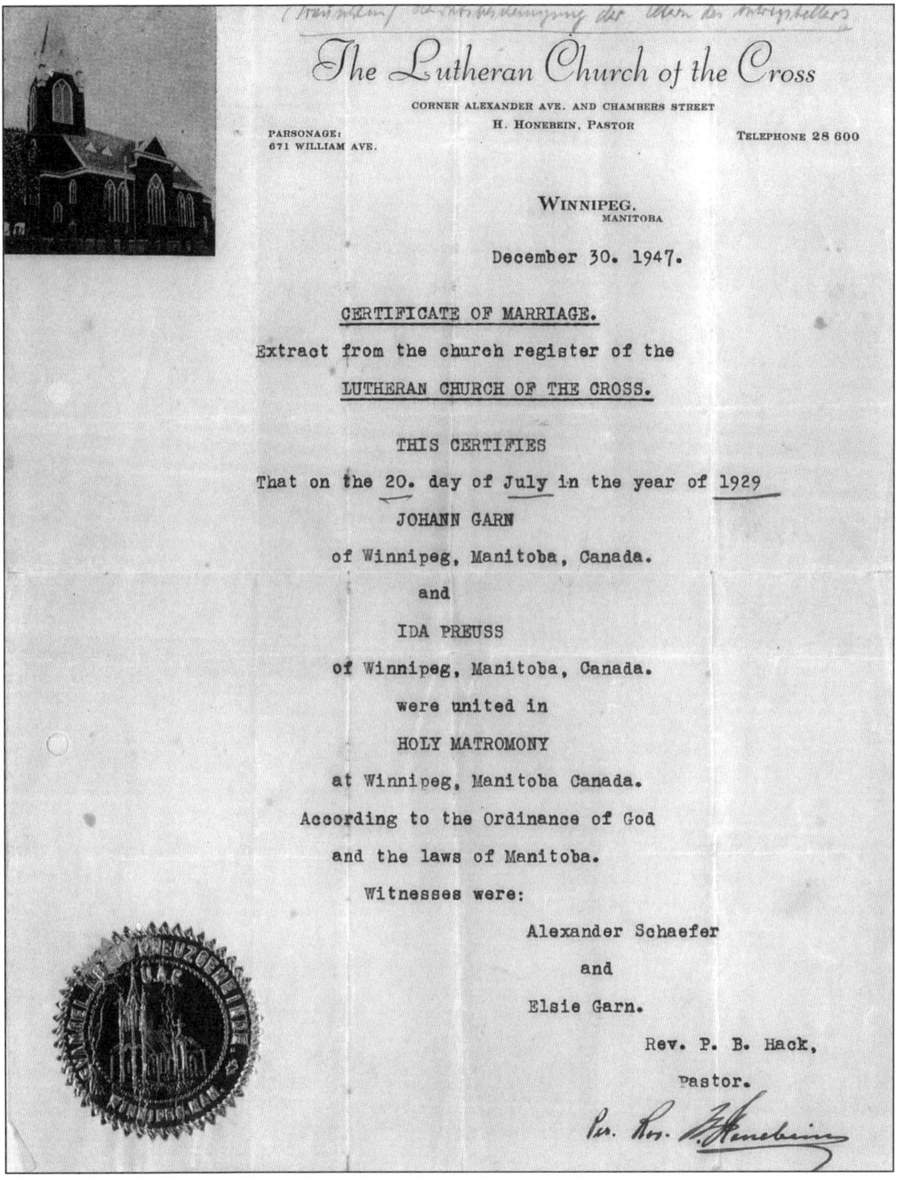

The Lutheran Church of the Cross

CORNER ALEXANDER AVE. AND CHAMBERS STREET

PARSONAGE:
671 WILLIAM AVE.

H. HONEBEIN, PASTOR

TELEPHONE 28 600

WINNIPEG,
MANITOBA

December 30. 1947.

CERTIFICATE OF MARRIAGE.

Extract from the church register of the

LUTHERAN CHURCH OF THE CROSS.

THIS CERTIFIES

That on the 20. day of July in the year of 1929

JOHANN GARN

of Winnipeg, Manitoba, Canada.

and

IDA PREUSS

of Winnipeg, Manitoba, Canada.

were united in

HOLY MATROMONY

at Winnipeg, Manitoba Canada.

According to the Ordinance of God

and the laws of Manitoba.

Witnesses were:

Alexander Schaefer

and

Elsie Garn.

Rev. P. B. Hack,

Pastor.

Mama and Papa's wedding certificate.

Harry and I in Winnipeg in 1934.

Our family in 1935 in Winnipeg.

Mama's passport photo
in preparation for our
return to Germany.

CHAPTER 1
THE BEGINNING

This is where *my* story really begins......

I must tell you, of course, that it is difficult to remember much of my early years in Winnipeg. But, as I ponder it, bits and pieces of memory come back to me. In Winnipeg, I remember a house with a pretty garden and chickens in the yard. I have some memories of the bakery where Mama and Papa occasionally took us.In 1934, Mama and Papa lost our barn and four horses in a fire. They were thankful and relieved that the bakery was spared. They rebuilt the barn and bought new horses. They used the horses to deliver the bread to our customers. It was the time of the Great Depression. I, also, have memories of a huge ship and leaving Papa. I remember being very scared.

It was February of 1936. I was 4½ years old and we were returning to Germany to take over the farm my Mama inherited from my Opa. (While we were living in Winnipeg, my grandparents back in Germany sold their home place and moved to the city of Marienwerder. But, Opa could not adjust to city life and bought another farm in Peterkau, West Prussia.) Papa stayed behind in Winnipeg a while longer so he could handle the final business arrangements concerning the bakery. So, Mama, Harry and I had to leave without him.

I can remember arriving in Germany, going to the farm and meeting my Opa and Oma for the very first time. I especially remember Opa Preuss. What I remember most about him was his moustache. It was huge with long handles that turned up at the tips. I can remember that I didn't want to kiss him! Not too long after this, he cut his moustache and wore it short and trimmed. He was very thin and tall. His hair was parted in the middle and was thin and grey for as long as I can remember. Opa had bought the farm with all the machinery and animals included. One of those animals was a short-tailed cat who ran and hid whenever he saw Harry and me. The animals were not used to kids! Opa and Oma Preuss lived with us on the farm and became a part of our happy family.

I vividly remember when Papa arrived a month later. How happy we were to see him! Papa was a kind, quiet and loving father who was rarely cross. He had a muscular, medium build and Harry and I loved to sit on his lap for hours and comb his wavy, coal black hair. When I was thirteen years old I would *still* sit on his lap and comb his hair. It seemed Mama was always working with her light brown, wavy hair pinned up at the back of her head in a bun. But, she was never too busy to be nice to everyone. She always seemed so thin…maybe from working so hard? When I was a child I always thought she was so tall, but she is actually just a little taller than I am now.

Now, the six of us became a family: Opa, Oma, Papa, Mama, Harry and me. We all had to make adjustments. Papa, who had been a baker, became a farmer. It was not easy for him. Harry and I had to adjust to the language. We had been speaking a mixed English/German. Harry had to attend school soon after we arrived and it was difficult for him to adapt. But, we were a happy family and happy to be back in our parents' native land!

CHAPTER 2
PETERKAU, WEST PRUSSIA

Our farm, as I remember it, was located in a valley near the town of Peterkau in West Prussia. The house was in a long building with the barn on one end and the house on the other. Even though they were connected, we still had to go around on the outside to get to the barn from the house. The whole structure was brick and quite old. I remember seeing the date, 1889, imprinted on one of the cornerstone bricks of the house. A year after we moved to our farm, Papa built a root cellar near the barn. A lovely flower garden surrounded the west end of the house. We, also, had lots of fruits and vegetables. Mama grew lots of currants, strawberries, raspberries and gooseberries. We had no electricity. There was a well in the back of the garden and a pump near the barn...this was our drinking water.

Our whole yard was filled with fruit trees. In fact, *all* the trees we had growing there were fruit trees, except for one huge birch tree. On the northwest side of the house the cherry trees were so big and tall the branches lay on the roof. The roof was flat and tarred and sometimes Harry and I would get permission to climb up on it so we could pick and eat the cherries that grew on the top most branches. They always seemed to taste better than the ones growing lower. And yet, we thought, the best cherries of all seemed to grow on the branches beyond our reach!

There was a gate in a tall wooden fence that separated the barnyard from the house and yard. We, often, forgot to close it and, then, the chickens would get into the garden. We would get such a scolding! So you see, we had the same problems and made the same mistakes you did when you were kids. Remember?

Our big dog, Mops, was chained in the barnyard. He was kind of like a guard dog and he and I never got along. I guess he didn't like kids either! It was a mutual understanding…I didn't like him and he didn't like me! When I had to feed him, I would set the food on the ground and push it towards him with a long stick. He always behaved as if he wanted to eat *me* instead! Of course, I didn't help the situation, either, by teasing him.

Our farm was small…about forty-eight acres. We did all the farm work with horses. We had two horses, but every other year, we would usually sell one in late fall after the work was all done, keeping our mare, Lotte, through the winter months. In early spring, she would give birth to a new colt. We had Lotte as long as we had the farm and every second spring we would have a new colt to break in. Harry and I had the most important job of all, to us anyway, which was to name the colts when they were born.

We had other animals on our farm, too. We usually kept about four cows and, also, chickens, geese and ducks. Mama would seldom raise turkeys because she said they ate too much. I can remember one year when we *did* have a turkey and Mama made her sit on some eggs she wanted to hatch. The turkey didn't want to sit, so she gave her a teaspoon of whiskey every day. And the turkey *sat!!!* After a few days the turkey would sit on the eggs all by herself without needing any whiskey. We had such fun with all the animals!

Of course, I had a pet, too. Her name was Nixe and she was more than a pet; she was my pal. She was a little white terrier with brown spots. Her face was brown with a little white blaze. She helped me herd the geese, just like Shep helped herd our cows. I was alone a lot, especially in the winter when Harry went to school, so Nixe became my playmate, too. We had such fun together. In the winter, Nixe and I would go sledding. I would wrap her in a blanket and put her in a box…you could only see her head sticking out. Then, I would put the box on a sled Papa had made for me and pull it around the yard. Sometimes I'd go over snow banks so quickly that the box fell off, but Nixe just lay there in her blanket until I picked up the box and put them both on the sled and away we'd go again!

In Germany, you have two choices regarding your education. After the first eight years of school, you may go to a trade school or, after passing exams at the end of grade four, you may attend Gymnasium (high school). After grade four, Harry chose to go to Gymnasium, seven kilometres³ away in Deutsch Eylau. In the summertime, he would ride his bike to and from school each day. But, in the winter, it was too cold, so he boarded with a family in town and only came home on the weekends. I went to school each morning at eight in Peterkau. We had a break at ten o'clock, when we'd eat a sandwich we'd brought from home. At one o'clock we were dismissed to go home. In the afternoon, the first three grades would have school from 1:00 to 4:00 p.m.. They had to split it this way because of the shortage of space and teachers. For you see, we were at war!

Every day two girls had to stay after school to scrape carrots and each day each child would receive a large carrot to eat. This was a required government programme that was instituted to ensure that every child got something healthy to eat each day. We had 165 students in our school and every day we scraped 165 carrots! We put them in cold water and the next day we passed them around in a big dishpan. Everyone got a carrot to eat and they were delicious! We had fun scraping them, too!

My Papa raised carrots on our farm and sold lots of them to the school. We raised other vegetables in our fields, too, and sold them in the market in Deutsch Eylau. We also grew wheat, rye, oats, barley, potatoes and rutabagas but, of course, compared to this country, the fields were small. But, when you have to do all the work either by hand or with horses, they seemed mighty big! Opa helped a lot with the fieldwork, although he didn't have to. He worked whenever he wanted to. I liked going to the fields and working with Opa. I'd rather do that any day then cook or clean in the house!

Opa and I were great pals! Sweet old Opa! He used to rescue me many times from a "licking" (spanking) I was going to get from Mama when I was naughty or lost a mitten. I used to lose so many mittens! (I still lose my mittens and gloves!) While Mama was "licking" me with a goose wing (usually used as a whiskbroom), I hoped that Opa would hurry and rescue me. He never let me down! He'd come in, not say a word, take my hand and go to his room and we would play Muehlchen (a German board game).

Our summers were mild and beautiful. Seldom did we have hot weather. Of course, if you were working in the fields while the sun was out you got quite hot. At night it always cooled off. The winters were very cold and sometimes we'd get a lot of snow. Spring usually arrived in March and it would get quite warm. We had many thunderstorms. When a storm ended we went outside to see if there were any lightening strikes. It was common to have two to three fires in the neighbourhood each year. I was very afraid of thunderstorms!

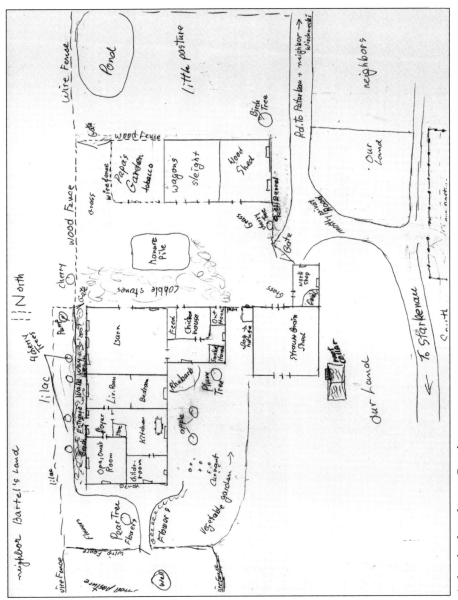

A sketch of our farm in Peterkau.

In front our house on our farm in Peterkau with Mama's relatives.

Me at eight years old.

Harry and I at a friend's home in Peterkau in 1941.

Harry at twelve years old.

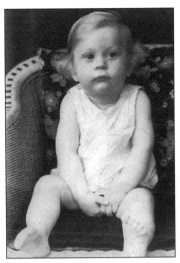
Herbert at one year old in 1944.

Papa

A poster that translates to "For Freedom and Life"…my Papa was a member of this military group called the Volkssturm.

Our last letter from Papa when he was on the Russian front, dated January 18, 1945. We fled our farm on January 20th.

CHAPTER 3

RUMBLINGS OF WAR

World War II began on September 1, 1939. Because we lived only twelve kilometres from the Polish border, we experienced, first hand, the beginning of the war. We saw fighter planes flying into Poland in such large groups they would darken the whole sky. We felt the ground shaking from the nearby cannon fire and heard the booming of the cannons the first day…then, it was silent. The war with Poland ended after a few days.

The following years, the war with Russia escalated. Many men, horses and dogs were being drafted into the military. Food and clothing shortages, as well as rationing of staples had begun. But, sadly, most deeply felt, were the thousands of fathers, husbands, brothers and sons who lost their lives on the front line. Since we had no radio or electricity, Mama and Papa went to the neighbor's home to listen to the latest war news and to follow the progress of the German troops who were advancing into Russia and were now in Stalingrad.

On July 4, 1943,when I was twelve years old, my baby brother, Herbert was born. Oh, how we spoiled him! He was the sunshine of our family with his blond, curly hair. He was such a chubby, happy baby!

In the fall of 1943, we received news that Mama's youngest brother, Uncle Walter, was killed in action. What indescribable pain! What anguish! Many had to experience this pain. Onkel Walter was Herbert's godfather and the last time we saw him was at Herbert's Baptism in August.

During the third week of December, Herbert became very ill. He lay in his little bed burning up with fever. Mama made cold compresses and laid them on his legs and arms, but it didn't help him. A doctor was called and he came out from Deutsch Eylau. He said Herbert had pneumonia. The only thing he could do for him was to give him an injection and we were told to wet his lips and put drops of water into his mouth. We, and the doctor, waited for his fever to break. Through the night of December 23rd, we were up all night in prayer, not knowing if Herbert would live until morning. When he opened his eyes, we realized his fever had finally broken. He looked at us and we hugged his weak, limp little body and covered him with kisses. The doctor gave us some medicine that we should continue to give him and, then, he left to return to the city. It was now December 24th. Papa went into the woods and returned with a lovely little Christmas tree about a metre tall. He put it up on the table and we decorated it with little pieces of white cotton batting. It was so beautiful and looked so pure. It represented the miracle God gave us in making our dear little five-month-old brother well.

During the winter of 1943 to 1944, a change took place at the Russian Front. The Russians were able to push the advancing German forces back. They continued to push them back well into the following year with hundreds of thousands killed. None of us believed that the retreat could continue across the border back into Germany. We believed the Germans would still be able to make a stand and push the Russians back once again. Sadly, this did not happen.

During the summer of 1944, the Russians advanced to the German border and, in some areas, began to cross the border into German territory. As word came that the Russians were quickly approaching the German border, all older men who originally had been too old to be drafted were now being called for active duty. They were first drafted to dig trenches for the ground troops. These troops of older men were called Volkssturm. And so my Papa was called to go, as well. He was gone from July to October. In exchange for his services, the military gave us an English prisoner-of-war to help us with the harvest. His name was Herbert; he was from London and could not speak a word of German. Luckily, Mama could speak some English, so they were able to communicate quite well. Herbert was incarcerated in a small prison for British soldiers working in the area of Peterkau. The British prisoners of war were guarded but, as long as no one escaped, the gate to the prison yard was left open so they could come and go as they pleased.

When Papa came home in October, we were allowed to keep the prisoner-of-war, Herbert, a while longer to help with farm work as Papa thought he would be called to serve again. One night when we were supposed to be sleeping, we overheard Papa tell Mama that things did not look good. They talked about when the war would be moving into our area and tried to decide what they should do. Harry and I were panic-stricken, but we kept it to ourselves, not saying anything to our parents. Soon afterward, Mama began packing most of our clothing and other belongings into big boxes. She left by train to deliver them to her cousins, the Fennings, who lived in Greifswalde, Pommern. This way, if the war reached our farm and we would have to suddenly leave, we wouldn't lose everything we owned. Mama was away for a couple of days, while we stayed on the farm with Opa.

I remember feeling so afraid. Everyone spoke in hushed voices and whispers, which scared us even more. They were saying how bad things looked for Germany. With winter arriving and Harry living and going to school in Deutsch Eylau, I would lay many evenings in bed worrying about all the things that could happen. One morning when I went to school, the kids said the Russians were in our country. The grown-ups wouldn't talk to the children about it. We were petrified!

Before we knew it, Christmas was upon us. I remember that we had a lot of snow before the holidays. Papa came home for Christmas and so did Harry. We had two weeks off from school so we played and went sledding like we had always done before and we were actually able to shut out of our minds what could happen in our future. Everything *seemed* perfect… just as if there wasn't a war raging. In the back of our minds we thought without a doubt that the German army would push the Russians right back over the border again. Fear and worry filled all of our thoughts day and night…and what about Christmas? Not one family member can remember Christmas that year.

After the Christmas holidays, Harry returned to school in Deutsch Eylau and the war became more of a reality. Papa received a letter saying that he would have to return to the military again…only this time it would be to fight rather than to dig trenches. We had only three more days together before he had to leave. But Papa wasn't the only one…all the other men in our village received the same notice. I remember how all the people gathered together that evening at the schoolhouse to discuss the possibility of an evacuation in case the war would come close to our area. Instructions were passed out as to which direction each township should go and the route to follow to the west. This would be all the more difficult and urgent as there would be only three men left in our whole township; the mayor and two officials from his office.

I shall never forget those last three days with my Papa before he left! He was so quiet, except to tell us over and over to be sure we always stayed together no matter what and to take care of each other. Because Harry was away at school, he couldn't even say good-bye to him. On the day he left, Papa came in my room early in the morning. I woke up as he bent over me to kiss me good-bye. I could feel his tears falling on my face. Very quietly, he walked out and I heard him say to Mama, "Promise me you will always take care of the kids." I didn't know then that those would be the last words I would ever hear him say. Mama walked with him a short way to the bahnhof (train station). This all took place on the tenth of January 1945.

Soon after that, preparations were made quietly, but quickly, for an evacuation. We were given a list telling us what to pack and how to pack it. Opa had fled during the First World War and knew more about what we should do than the officials did who were directing us. But, as we were doing all of this we were still hoping that we wouldn't really have to leave.

On the twelfth of January, we began to hear the rumbling of the cannons. At first, nobody said anything about it. Everyone was too afraid to mention it. But on the following day when they became significantly louder, the people started to hold meetings in town and Opa and Mama went. There, they were told that the Nazi regime would *not* lose the war and Germany would be able to turn the invasion around. When they returned from the meeting, they told me that maybe we wouldn't have to be gone for very long or have to go very far if we *did* have to leave. Believing that we would be able to return soon made the prospect of leaving easier to bear.

On January 13th and 14th, the rumbling of the guns seemed fainter and we all *hoped* everything was going to turn out okay. In fact, all our normal duties and routines continued as if nothing had changed or as if nothing was going to happen. I still went to school every day during this time and we, also, shipped our milk each day. On the 15th and 16th we even threshed the grain we had harvested the summer before. (It was common practice in Germany, at that time, to harvest the grain in August and store the bundles in a shed until wintertime. Then, the farmers would thresh it, separating the grain from the stalks, when they had more time.) The weather was bitter cold and the air was so still you could hear the bombs exploding from many kilometres away.

On the 17th of January, Herbert, our prisoner-of-war had to leave. The guard, who was in charge of the prisoners-of-war, ran to our farm early in the morning and said they had to leave at once! Suddenly, it was HURRY! HURRY! After he left, we all sensed the sudden urgency and became frightened again. Opa checked the horses' harnesses to be sure they were in good shape. He had to fit a harness for Lore, one of our horses. Poor Lore!! Because she was only two years old she hadn't been harness trained yet. This bothered Opa and Mama as they worried about how she would manage in one.

The time had actually come. Opa and our closest neighbor, Paul Wischnewski, worked together getting the wagons ready to travel. To make our wagon longer, they put an extension pole in the centre under the wagon to lengthen the wheelbase. Next, the wagons were packed. Mama and I had already packed most of our winter clothing, blankets, pillows and feather beds. All the food was packed towards the bottom of the wagon. Mama even packed some fruit, vegetables and meat she had canned. She placed these jars into boxes and put them in the wagon, too. Harry and I were to be confirmed on the 18th of March and all the relatives were expected to be there, so Mama packed canned items that had been kept especially for the Confirmation. Also, Opa and Mama butchered a pig, wrapped it up and packed it in the bottom of the back end of the wagon. We had to be sure to take oats along for the horses. To ensure our survival, it was just as important for them to eat and stay strong.

By the time we had everything prepared, it was January 18th. Harry was to come home from Deutsch Eylau so we could all leave together. Mama became more worried each day that he did not return home. Deutsch Eylau was a larger city and would be hit by the war before we would. When he hadn't returned home by noon on the 18th, Mama was frantic and said someone would have to go get him, since she felt he probably didn't have a way to get home. Opa couldn't go because he was very busy working on the wagon and also, had to go to yet another meeting. So, that left *me*. I was quite good at handling the horses and Lotte was so gentle, anyone could handle her!

Right after dinner, Opa harnessed Lotte to our little sleigh.[4] Mama wrapped me up in blankets and gave me *strict* instructions to be very careful! She told me that I must remember to bring back the blankets and pillows Harry had at school because we would need them. I said 'okay'… and told them not to worry. Off I went and everything was going just fine. I felt proud that Mama thought I could do this all by myself. Of course, I *knew* I could do it; after all I was thirteen years old!!

It was a cloudy winter day and the roads were so quiet…scarcely anyone around. But, when I got to the main highway, it was chaos! Lotte wasn't afraid of cars, but was frightened of anything bigger than that. She had rarely seen a truck before and now we faced trucks *and* army tanks all over the highway. The highway was slippery and Lotte was so scared to walk on the ice. I had such a difficult time getting her to go. I had her walk along the edge where there was a little gravel and she wouldn't slip so easily. Trees lined the highway on both sides so I had to be very careful we didn't get hooked on a tree with the sleigh.

As I neared the city I met more and more of the German army coming from the front. Not only huge army trucks, but also, tanks and they were all moving quite fast. Suddenly, Lotte stopped and started backing up. By this time I was frantic. I was crying and praying that nothing would happen. I was so terrified that Lotte would fall and break something on her harness or the sleigh and, then, how would I ever find Harry and get back home! The war was coming so fast! You can't imagine all the absolutely horrible thoughts that went through my mind. I took the whip and started hitting Lotte in panic. She started to run! Oh, how thankful I was to God for helping me through those terrifying moments! Every time we approached a truck or tank I would whip Lotte frantically so she wouldn't stop. All this time I was crying and the tears were freezing on my cheeks. A big truck passed carrying a full load of soldiers and some civilians. Suddenly, I heard someone yelling from one of the trucks, "Ruth! Ruth!" I stopped Lotte and looked back to see one of the trucks stop and someone jump off. I shouted with joy! It was Harry! "Harry! Harry!" I started to cry. He jumped on the sleigh, took the reins and began to turn it around to go home, but, then, I remembered the blankets and pillows. Harry said we had better go get them.

As we drove into the city, I wished we had gone home instead. Lotte was so nervous and jumpy. The city was packed with army tanks, guns and cannons. It was chaos and confusion everywhere. There were many soldiers, but few civilians left. The army was setting up for the defence of the city and here we came with a horse and sleigh! The streets were jampacked and everything was so mixed up, such mayhem…soldiers, trucks, guns, tanks, cannons and people…one couldn't walk anywhere. The only route left open to us was the sidewalk, and there wasn't much snow for the sleigh there. Lotte had such a hard time pulling the sleigh on the cement. But we finally got to the school. Harry ran in and got the bedding while I stayed in the sleigh holding on to Lotte. As soon as he returned, we hastily left town. It was a lot easier going back because we were going in the same direction as all the trucks and traffic. Lotte knew she was going home and she wanted to run all the way!

On our way back we came to a forest. There was a road through it that Opa sometimes used because it was a shortcut. Harry thought we should take it so we could get away from all the army vehicles and pandemonium, but I was scared that we would get lost since neither of us had gone that way before. Harry went anyway. It would have been such a pleasant trip through the woods if it hadn't been for the war. It was so beautiful!! The road was narrow…just enough room for the sleigh to pass through. The snow was smooth and shimmering and so soft looking…like clouds. Overhead the branches hung low over the road, laden with their beautiful burdens of snow. Every once in awhile we would see a bird fly here and there and see the tracks of some small animal in the snow. Here there was no sign of the war. It was so quiet and peaceful! The sleigh bells echoed sounding as if there were hundreds of them. Lotte quieted down to a steady pace and everything seemed calm and safe. When we came to the crossroads and forks in the road, we just let the reins hang loose and hoped and prayed that Lotte would choose the right way to go. Soon we came to a clearing and recognized the countryside and the Sportplatz,[5] we thanked the Lord and Lotte, too, for showing us the way home.

We hurried home then…it had taken us three hours. Mama and Opa were so happy to see us. They just kept hugging us and hugging us over and over again. Opa had the wagon all ready to go and we just had to wait for the command from the officials to be able to leave.

The next day was Friday, January 19th. We were ready to go and, by this time, resigned to leaving. We got up early in the morning and I remember all of us standing outside listening for a sign or signal of some sort that meant we could go. The sun was shining, but it was very cold. The big flakes of snow that lay on the ground sparkled like thousands of diamonds. We could hear dogs barking in the distance and somebody hammering (perhaps making last minute adjustments to their wagons or sleighs), and off and on we'd hear sleigh bells jingling. Everything looked so beautifully white with snow and wonderfully but, eerily still. The officials told us we would have to wait until we get the order to leave in a group. The order didn't come. The whole time we were waiting, the ground was vibrating from the cannon and gunfire. We knew the Russians were near.

Suddenly, someone shouted from one of the sleighs on a distant road that one of us was to go into town. I can't remember whether Mama or Opa went, but there they were told that we were to leave Saturday morning, the 21st of January. We were to meet in the centre of town. Orders were given that all cattle were to be left tied up in the barns. The Volkssturm would come by later in the middle of the day, untie them and take them away in large herds throughout the area. They, also, told us and the other refugees which route we were to take.

On Saturday morning, January 21, 1945, we got up early, milked the cows and fed the animals. Mama made sure we dressed in very warm clothing. We put on our oldest and *biggest* shoes because we were wearing three pair of wool socks. In fact, we had on several pairs of everything from warm underwear to a couple dresses and heavy slacks and jackets, a cap and scarf and two pair of mittens. Mama placed her cherished two kilogram[6] bag of sugar inside a linen sack and placed it in the front of the wagon. Next, Opa and Mama harnessed Lotte and Lore. We had two horses. Lotte was the old, experienced mare we could count on, but Lore was a young two-year-old not yet broken in. Poor Lore! She was so frightened and nervous, her body just shook! Opa hooked the horses up and Mama and Herbert got on the wagon. Little Herbert was dressed really warm, too. Mama had wrapped him in a feather quilt. Herb was just eighteen months old and seemed so bewildered by all that was happening.

By the time we got started, the rumbling of the guns was so intense that the windows of our house clattered. After we left our yard, we passed Wischnewski's and saw their wagon was ready to go, too. We drove down the road and up the little hill. There, Opa stopped the horses for a minute and we all looked back at our home. Even though the guns were rumbling in the distance, our home still looked so quiet and peaceful...like a picture. The snow and frost on the trees was so beautiful. Our last look was more than we could bear. Mama wept so hard and we started to cry, too, as if our hearts would break.

Suddenly, I remembered Nixe!! Earlier that morning while we were getting ready to go I had wondered where she had gone to. But, then, in the rush and excitement I had forgotten to go look for her. Oh, how I wanted my Nixe! I begged and begged to be allowed to run back and find her. Mama said, "No!" but she *did* let Harry run back to conduct a quick search. He looked all over the house and barn. He called and called, but there was no sign of Nixe. He came back without her. I was so sad; I thought my heart would surely break. All I could do was pray that whoever let the cattle out of the barn, would give her something to eat or would take her with them and take care of her. We couldn't wait any longer to see whether she would turn up. Lore was getting more and more nervous and wouldn't stand still anymore. We had to climb back onto the wagon and start our journey to town.

Once in town, all the wagons were to form a wagon train so we could all leave in an orderly fashion. However, when we got to town, we thought we were too early as we didn't see anyone around. Suddenly, we spotted another wagon. When it came nearer we saw that it was the Wischnewski's. How we shouted to get their attention! They told us that they just discovered that everybody had left already. They didn't know how long ago, but the village was deserted and empty. They must have left the evening before or, even, during the night. All had left without the order to do so…the order never came. We found out later that the officials had fled the evening before and had a whole night's head start. We didn't waste another minute. We hurried out of the village towards the highway we would have to take to escape. Lotte and Lore must have sensed the urgency, for they wanted to take off and so we let them run. Lore was no trouble at all and drove so well. We were very thankful, for it wasn't easy pulling such a heavily loaded wagon through the snow.

In about a half-hour we reached the highway. There, we had to stop. We could not believe what we saw!! As far as we could see, the highway was a solid mass of wagons, horses and people. We had to wait a long time before we were able to squeeze into a slight opening to become a part of that massive sea of humanity fleeing the guns and an enemy we hadn't seen…but we could hear ever more loudly. This long string of fleeing refugees and their wagons, later, became known as the "treck."

Some refugees. *Bundesarchiv. Bild 175-S00-00326, o.Ang., 1945*

An example of the treck. *Bundesarchiv.*
Bild 137-065321, Wisniewski, 1940

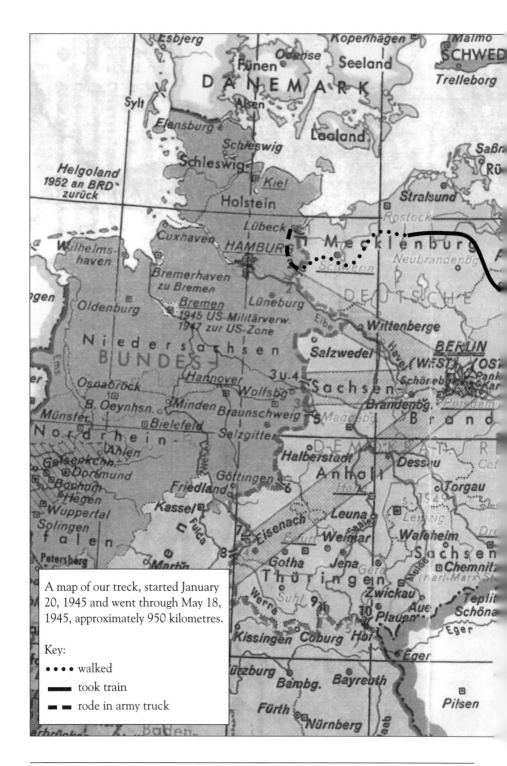

A map of our treck, started January 20, 1945 and went through May 18, 1945, approximately 950 kilometres.

Key:

•••• walked

▬▬ took train

■ ■ rode in army truck

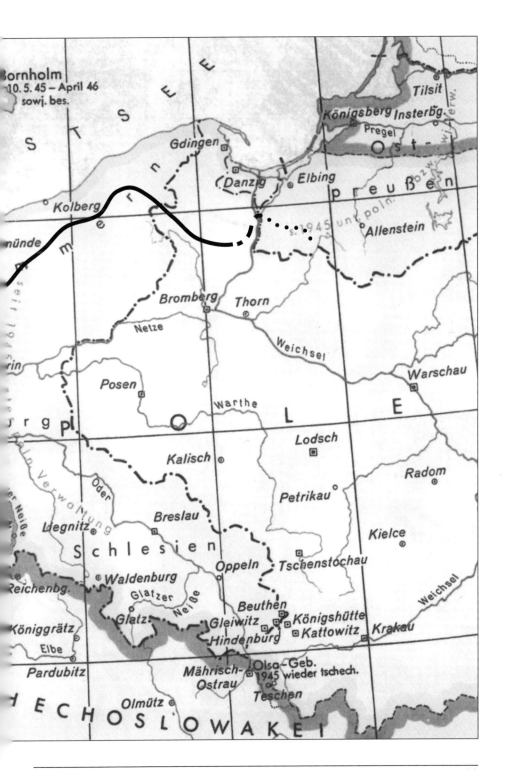

Bornholm
10.5.45 – April 46
sowj. bes.

S T S E E

O S T S E E

Königsberg Insterbg. Tilsit

Pregel

Gdingen

Danzig Elbing p r e u ß e n

1945 unt poln.

Allenstein

Kolberg

münde

Bromberg Thorn

Netze

Weichsel

rin

Warschau

Posen

Warthe

O L E

r g pl

Lodsch

Kalisch

Oder

Radom

Petrikau

Breslau

Liegnitz

S c h l e s i e n

Kielce

er Neiße

Verwaltung

Oppeln Tschenstochau

Waldenburg

Reichenbg. Glatzer

Neiße

Beuthen

Königgrätz Glatz Gleiwitz Königshütte

Hindenburg Kattowitz Krakau

Elbe

Weichsel

Pardubitz Mährisch- Olsa-Geb.
Ostrau 1945 wieder tschech.

Teschen

Olmütz

H E C H O S L O W A K E I

Our wagon looked a lot like this one does. *Bundesarchiv.*
Bild 146-1996-030-01A, Höber, Brigitte, Februar 1945

More refugees and soldiers on the treck. *Bundesarchiv. Bild 146-1976-072-09, o.Ang., Februar-März 1945*

The refugees used a variety of materials to make shelters on the tops of the wagons. *Bundesarchiv. Bild 183-W0402-500, Dissmann, Juli 1944*

Many refugees used blankets to make shelters on their wagons… we did too. *Bundesarchiv. Bild 137-051846, Spahn, B., 1940*

Sadly, along the way many, many people and animals lost their lives. *Bundesarchive. Bild 146-1990-001-30, o.Ang., 1945*

An example of what the cities and towns looked like after the bombings. *Bundesarchiv. Bild 183-J31345, o.Ang., Februar-März 1945*

CHAPTER 4
THE TRECK

Lotte and Lore could not run here. We crawled along at a snail's pace. We began to feel the bitter cold, so we got off the wagon and started walking to get warm. It must have been way past lunchtime already, so we ate some sandwiches Mama had packed. Luckily they weren't frozen yet and we drank some hot chicory[7] coffee. Little Herb had his bottle, too. Because we frequently came to a standstill, often up to two or more hours, we had no problems eating or drinking and we could run into abandoned farmsteads to heat our coffee and still catch up to our wagon.

What a commotion! As we were fleeing west, the German army was travelling on the same road heading in the same direction. Here and there, a wagon would have to drop out of the treck because an axle would break or something else would go wrong with their wagon. Then, it was very difficult for them to get back into the *treck* again. It was interesting to see how people prepared for this unwanted journey. Some had brought their dogs along and others had decided to bring a cow along so they would have some milk for their children. They would tie her to the back of their wagon where she would be pulled along. I shuddered with pity for the poor cow whose feet were bloodied from walking so long in the cold and with only the snow-covered ground to lie on when the wagons were at a standstill. If a person or an animal died, the body was laid in the ditch. If it were a dead child, the mother would wrap a blanket around the child's body and lay it under a tree or a bush. The same was done with an aged mother or father. We would watch all this in horror and disbelief. The grief of the families would break our hearts. But, to save everyone else's life, the treck had to keep moving despite the tragedies…you didn't dare lose your place in line. It was here, just before Riesenburg, that we saw soldiers pulling small sleds carrying wounded comrades to a Lazarett (military hospital) in Riesenburg.

By evening, horses and people alike were exhausted. Refugees began to drop out of the line and pull into deserted farmyards where they hoped to find shelter from the cold night and give their weary animals a rest. We, also, drove into a yard where some other wagons had already stopped. It was deserted, the owners having left a long time ago. The people went through the pantries and basement looking for something to eat. How welcome it was to build a fire and have something hot to eat. The horses were put in the barn and given oats and hay left behind by the farm's owners. Everyone tried to get some sleep. At least the children did, but I wonder how much sleep Mama and Opa had. I'm sure they lay awake a long time wondering and worrying about what tomorrow would bring.

We got up early the next morning. After searching the pantry and finding some food for our breakfast, we fed the horses and were back on the road. Some families never stopped. If they didn't have a baby or elderly person with them they kept going day and night. This time we didn't have as much trouble getting back on the highway and finding a place in the treck. It was Sunday now, but few of us were aware of it. Time didn't mean much to us except how far we could travel from sun-up to sundown, putting as many kilometres between the enemy and us as possible. Few of us had clocks. Our stomachs and the position of the sun told us when it was time to eat and when it was time to rest. Our biggest concern was staying warm and just trying to move forward instead of stopping so much. We, also, lived with the daily fear that the German army would come and confiscate our horses. They needed horses badly and when they found them, they would take them from the treck.

Around noon, some men on foot began passing us, coming from the front lines, (which was the direction from which we were fleeing). As they passed by, they looked each wagon over carefully. The wagons were at a standstill so often that it was easy for them to overtake and pass us. More and more came as the afternoon passed and by evening we had found out who they were. They were the older men of all the villages and towns who had been drafted into the *Volkssturm*, the same group that Papa belonged to. We began to see men from our village, Peterkau, and from other neighboring villages. We anxiously looked for Papa to be among the next group we'd see. We counted the men from our village as they passed. And always we said, in our hearts, if not with our lips, that the next one would be our Papa.

But, it was always someone else. Mama began asking the men if they had seen Papa, but no one would tell her anything. After the last of the men had stopped coming, there were only two men from Peterkau who were not amongst them…Otto Schulz and Papa. As we walked alongside the wagon, Mama sobbed, broken-hearted, because she knew Papa was never coming back.

That evening when we pulled into yet another deserted farmyard, by Dakau, to find shelter for the night, we were so happy to discover that amongst the other families that had stopped, there were some people we knew from Peterkau. You can imagine how overjoyed Harry and I were to see some of our classmates again. It brought a bit of home to us.

After finding food to eat (Grandpa always made sure the horses had something to eat, too!), Harry and I, with our reunited friends, went sledding on a hill nearby with sleds we found in the farmyard. For a short, glorious time that night we just had fun and forgot there was a war and that we were a long way from our home.

That night the weather deteriorated. It was dreary and the temperature was dropping, making our situation the next day much more critical. The first two nights we were fortunate enough to find farms where the owners had left their cows tied in the barn. Everyone who stayed there fed them and, in return, had milk to drink. Mama would save some milk for Herbert during the day when we were fleeing but, now it was so bitterly cold, the milk froze. Harry would take the milk bottle and run ahead to the next farm to see if he could find a way to warm it for baby Herbert.

When we stopped to rest that third night, we discovered much to our dismay, that the owners of this farm had let the cows run loose in the barnyard. He had feared the poor animals would get nothing to eat if they were tethered in the barn. The cows ran up to us bellowing in pain because of their hard, swollen udders. When we would try to milk them, they would run away in pain. At last we gave up and went into the house where at least we could get warm. We wondered what we would eat that night. Mama checked the canned jars we had brought along in the wagon, but all were frozen and most were broken. We could salvage very little. But that bag of sugar became a blessing because she made sugar water to give to Herbert to drink. It was becoming more and more difficult to find food as many in the treck ahead of us were hungry, too.

The weather was not only freezing cold but, now; the wind began blowing harder and harder. Opa and the other men of the families that had stopped, went out and began to construct some sort of shelter over the wagons to protect us the next day. With some lumber they found they built a walled shelter on top of the wagons and nailed blankets over the top (with an opening in the front). These resembled the covered wagons of the Old West except these were pointed like a tent rather than with the gently rounded tops. They worked late in the night getting the wagons ready.

The next morning, our fourth day, the sky was hazy. This misty haze had frozen and the highway was covered with a thin sheet of ice. It was dangerously slippery. If that weren't bad enough, we had to begin this day with nothing to eat or drink. Mama wrapped Herbert in an old fur coat she had remembered to throw into the wagon, a fur coat she had when she still lived in Canada…which seemed an eternity ago.

This was a bad, bad day. We passed many wagons that had broken down and people were frantically trying to fix them. We saw horses that had fallen on the ice and were injured. Some had broken their harnesses. It was terrible. One man was trying to keep people from going around him because he was afraid he would lose his place in this treck of escaping humanity and be left behind forever. No one stopped to help him. Everybody had the same gnawing dread of losing their place and being left behind, unable to find another spot. Time was running out. The rumbling of the guns was becoming louder and louder.

Soon we came to a steep hill which, covered in ice, became a death trap. Some of the people had made a run for it hoping to get enough momentum to get to the top. But halfway up the horses began slipping and falling. The drivers, panicking, began to hit and whip them. Some of the wagons turned crossways blocking the road completely. Some got stalled trying to go around these wagons. Everywhere horses lay injured with a broken leg or other injury. Everywhere we looked there was death and agony. Animals shrieking in pain…agony and horror…plus our fear of the rapidly approaching enemy armies. I will never forget this day. How those stalled people ever found a way out of their predicament, I shall never know. Suddenly, one wise farmer decided to get off the highway and reach the top of the hill via the fields, returning to the highway at the top. After he made it, everyone else, seeing his success followed behind him. As people went along preparing to make it up this hill and others, they unloaded their wagons with everything they could possibly get along without. This was done in order to lighten up the loads…this unloading of belongings continued throughout the journey. When Harry had to go ahead in search of new farms and cows for milk for Herbert, he would look in the ditch and almost always find a bicycle to use. When he came back, he left it wherever we were because he knew he would, more than likely, find another one further up the road again.

It was becoming more and more difficult to find overnight places to stay because, as the days went by, there were more and more refugees ahead of us as people continually joined the evacuation from many other areas. Often we spent the night sleeping in a chair. But, at least, we still had shelter from the outdoors and the cold. It was equally as hard on the horses. Poor, poor Lore! She was not used to having a harness on her and had been wearing one for days now pulling the heavy wagon and us, too. She was rubbed raw and bleeding from the strap on her chest and the bit of the bridle in her mouth. Opa would use a halter instead of the bit and bridle for her tender, bleeding mouth. He would put a soft cloth between her body and the strap on the harness that rubbed her chest raw.

Four days had gone by and the rumbling guns were getting louder and louder. Conditions on the road continued to worsen and deadly apathy began to affect the refugees who were becoming worn out and discouraged. Some turned around and started back and some, not being able to go forward or backward another step, just stayed at the last farmstead they reached and waited for whatever might befall them.

By this time, we thought if we could just drive through the night when most of the wagons had stopped, we could get ahead. We decided to try it. We kept driving into the night and it got colder and colder. Someone came along and told Mama that a few kilometres down the road and off to the side was a school. There, the Red Cross was taking care of sick people and had food for children and adults who were sick or had babies. Mama thought we should try to get there. We decided we would get there faster if we walked ahead without the wagon. Opa stayed in line with the wagon. While we walked, Mama carried Herbert. It was a long way, but soon we were inside the school. It was so blessedly warm! There were a lot of people. Straw had been strewn all over the floor and that's where the refugees lay. The Red Cross workers gave us soup and something hot to drink. Mama left us to go back to the wagon to be with Opa, but before she left she told us to stay there until she and Opa got to the school. We said "okay" and relaxed in the straw. Little Herbert cried a little and a lady talked to us. She was so nice. Soon we were fast asleep.

I don't know how long we had been asleep, when suddenly a loud explosion erupted. We woke up in a panic. The doors and windows had been blown out of the school. Plaster was falling down and everyone was screaming and crying. Refugees were running hysterically all over the place and almost, in a flash, they were all gone and the building was empty. They had fled to their wagons. We were left there all alone crying and scream-ing in terror, with no one left to hear us or help us. We did not know what to do. Harry said we had to go, too, so we grabbed Herbert and wrapped him in the fur coat. As we started to leave I was crying because I didn't want to go. I remembered what Mama had said about our remaining right there until she came for us. I was hysterical with fear. Harry, frightened and angry, was sobbing and yelled at me to "COME NOW!" because the building could collapse at any moment. He said, then, that we'd meet Mama on the road somewhere. I cried and wept frantically, saying, "How do you know we'll meet her if we don't even know where she is? There are thousands of people out there, she'll never see us!"

After he pushed and pulled me, we finally joined the masses of hu-manity walking towards the highway. We were almost there when we saw Mama running towards us crying hysterically. She grabbed us and hugged and hugged us. She told us how thankful she was that she had found us. She, then, said we had to hurry back to Opa and the wagon. The Russians were advancing and were very close. They were shooting with army tanks. Before we got to the wagon we saw Opa coming towards us. He told us that the treck was at a standstill and if we were going to be able to get away at all, we would have to walk. He drove the wagon into the woods, took the bridles off the horses and gave them a big tub of oats. He left them there and came back carrying only the bag of sugar. By this time it was beginning to get daylight.

We walked and walked and walked. When we got too hungry, we would try to find something to eat at abandoned farms and homes along the way. Later in the afternoon, Mama was staggering and finally sat down by a hedge along the road. She was sobbing and her body shook with complete exhaustion. She was so weary and her arms ached from carrying Herbert so long. Her legs and knees were worn out. Mama had reached the point where nothing mattered anymore. She just wanted to sit there and not take one more step. Opa, too, was aching and exhausted. He, also, had reached that state of apathy where nothing mattered anymore. They both said, "Let the Russians roll over us!" But, God in His mercy must have been prodding us children with a sense of the danger and urgency to proceed. Crying and begging we pleaded with them to go on. We were so frightened. With God's help, we pulled and pulled and got Mama back on her feet. Once more we were on our way.

When night came we arrived at a place that looked like a deserted Gasthaus.[8] There, we found something hot to drink. Mama was so tired. She had to have some rest and sleep before we could go on. We had to sleep in straight-back chairs with our heads resting on the backs and Herbert sleeping on the floor beneath Mama's feet. Mama just sat there looking around at all the people. Every once in awhile she would get up and check some man who was slouched over in his sleep in a chair. She was still always looking for Papa. Maybe, just maybe, it would be him. Finally, we slept. Although it was still dark, we awoke because it was very noisy with people coming and going. We thought we better get started walking again. We were able to get some hot broth to drink and found a bottle for Herbert. We still had the old nipple from his old bottle and put it on this one. Mama's knees were so swollen; they looked and felt like large water bags. Opa looked around and found a long leather belt, which he fashioned into a sling around Herbert. He strapped him onto Mama so even though she had to put her arms around him to keep him warm, she no longer had to bear his whole weight with her arms.

As they were doing this, Mama and Opa were talking with some of the people who were there. They told us some gruesome tales of what happened to those people who had turned back. They had seen some of these poor people shot to death by the Russians and the women raped to death in front of their children. Those parting words to us were an incentive for us, if at all possible, to continue to go forward. Do not linger. Do not stop. Do not turn back. We were terrified!

We were soon on the highway again. Because we were on foot, we did not have to fight for a spot in the *treck*, which had been standing still for a long time, not going anywhere. Soon we were passing the wagons. Ahead, at a spur or fork in the road, our Army was coming onto the highway ahead of us and the *treck* had to wait until the army went first. As we watched the army trucks roll onto the road, Mama talked with one of the officers. He told her if we wanted to make it through, we would have to walk very quickly because that night they planned to blow up the bridge that crossed the Weichsel River so that the Russians couldn't cross it. This was a very wide river and the bridge was the only way across; for us and for the armies. If we didn't make it across the river, we would be stuck. If we did make it across, it would increase our chances of getting ahead of the Russians.

So, we walked even faster even though we were so tired! All afternoon we walked or, rather, ran along the top of the dyke that held back the Weichsel River. We walked past people we recognized from neighboring villages back home and wondered how they had gotten so far with their wagons when we had abandoned ours three days ago. They must have left home long before we did, or else kept travelling through the nights. We didn't stop for anything, not even to eat. Opa was exhausted and becoming very weak so Harry and I supported him on each side to keep him moving. No matter how weary we were we all took turns carrying that bag of sugar, because no matter what happened, Mama said to hang on to that bag of sugar! That little bag held life for us when there was no other food available. The closer we got to the bridge, the wider the river became. Suddenly we could see the bridge in the distance and along with it masses of humanity, including the German army, fleeing towards it.

There were several highways converging at the bridge and the military police were directing traffic…first one highway of people and wagons went for awhile and then another. The refugees were pushing and shoving to get across the bridge. We learned later that several wagons decided that they would not wait in the line-up to cross and attempted to cross the Weichsel River, hoping the ice would support them. It was okay for the first wagon, but when others saw it cross they followed and the weight of so many caused the ice to break away. Wagons, horses and people all broke through the ice and went under the water. It was terrible. The horses screamed in panic and pain trying to escape the deadly cold water and ice. A few people were able to crawl out onto ice floes and were carried downstream. Were they ever rescued or did they float out into the Baltic Sea? Many people and animals perished from drowning and hypothermia that day.

The Red Cross was there, too, and before we went across the bridge they gave us some hot chicken soup. It was so thinned down, it was almost all water, but to us it was the best chicken soup we had ever tasted in our whole life. It was late afternoon before we crossed the bridge. We crossed with tears in our eyes and a prayer of thanks to the Lord in our hearts.

After crossing the bridge we were in a quandary as to where we should go from there. By this time, the directions we had received when we left home meant nothing. It was 'every man for himself.' We were in a little town on the other side and there were army trucks everywhere. Mama asked one of the soldiers where they were headed. He told her that they were going straight north to Danzig and offered us a ride with them and maybe, then, we could get on a ship at Danzig to cross the Baltic Sea to western Germany. He said they were evacuating Danzig by ship.

That sounded like the best thing for us to do, so we climbed in the back of the open truck box. Oh, how good it felt to sit down! But something went wrong. We waited and waited and the truck still had not moved. Finally, Harry went and found the soldier Mama had talked to and asked why we weren't moving. He told us the truck had engine trouble and they were trying to repair it.

After waiting what seemed an eternity, and being thoroughly chilled to the bone, we thought we better get off and start walking. Mama was so stiff from sitting that, at first, she couldn't even move. A road sign pointed to the town of Preussisch-Stargard and it was about fifty kilometres away. Since we knew it was a considerably bigger city and we would be moving south, we decided we would try to get there. But Mama just couldn't walk anymore. So Opa and Harry said they would start walking and try to hitch a ride along the way. If someone picked them up they'd have them come back for us. We were really afraid of splitting up, in case we didn't find each other again, but we could see no other way to solve this dilemma. So, with prayers in our hearts and on our lips that we would see them again… they left.

At this time, Mama spotted our neighbor's wagon sitting nearby. On it sat old Grossmutter[9] Kaminski, Herr[10] Kaminski's mother, hungry, very confused and nearly frozen to death. She said that Leo and Meta went to find some food a long time ago and never came back. Mama knew she must have been sitting there for a long time because the horses had dug out a big hole by scratching into the ground with their front hooves (horses do this when they stand too long). Mama went to the back of their wagon to see if there might be some bread to eat, but when she lifted the blanket she discovered Frau Kaminski's father, old Grossvater[11] Redner, dead. She was so shocked. She put the blanket back down and walked away. Mama thinks they were left there to die. We saw this happen so often along our journey. The sick, disabled or elderly who couldn't keep up were left behind, so the stronger and more able would have a chance at survival. When despair and horror befalls you, it can drive you to do those things when it comes to saving your own life.

As we waited for Harry and Opa to return, we talked with some of the soldiers and one of them said he was leaving for Preussisch-Stargard and that we could have a ride. So once again we climbed in the back of an Army truck. Mama told the soldiers who were driving; that Opa and Harry had gone ahead and that if we saw them they would have to stop and pick them up. He said to just be sure and signal him and he would stop. We hadn't gone too far down the highway when we saw Harry and Opa walking ahead of us. We pounded on the roof of the truck so hard we thought it would break. Our driver stopped and Harry and Opa jumped on, we were overjoyed that we were all together once again. As we started up again, we saw herds of cattle being chased by some men. They looked as cold and hungry as we were. We thought, maybe, those were the cattle from back home. But Mama told us she talked with some people along the way from Peterkau and they had found cattle choked to death in the abandoned barns. No one had come to untie them and as the hunger pains and thirst overcame them, they ended up strangling themselves. Man and beast alike suffered the agonies of war.

The truck left us at a railway station about half way to Preussisch-Stargard. The floor of the station was covered with straw and many people lay there resting. We found a spot to lie and cuddled close together for warmth. Near us lay a group of Vlassek soldiers ("White Russians" who fought on the German side). Opa talked with them. They gave us some food to eat and said they had family left in the Ukraine and had no idea how the "Red Russians" (communists) were treating them. They told Opa, they were fleeing from the same Russians as we all were. They said that if the "Red Russians" would ever catch up with us, they would shoot us, no questions asked.

In the morning, after a night's rest, we felt a little stronger and started walking. Shortly, some German soldiers picked us up again. We rode in the back of their truck until they left us at a school in Preussisch-Stargard... these soldiers, with the rest of the army already there, were setting up a military defence in the city. Here, again, we found the Red Cross feeding people and trying to give them shelter and a place to rest. Everyone was given some thin soup and buttered bread. They even had some milk for the babies. A lot of people were there. As in the other school we were in, there was straw spread over the floor, often in nice thick bunches and families huddled close together. We all lay on the straw and were so thankful for it.

We stayed there all night and wondered where we would go next. At times like this, I wondered what thoughts went through Mama's mind as she, alone, had the full responsibility of two children, an old man and a little baby weighing on her shoulders. What a heavy burden! No wonder she didn't want to go on anymore. The strain must have been unbearable. When morning came, she once more had reached that point where she didn't care if she went one step further. She was just too weary of it all. Her determination and will power were gone. But once again, Harry and I begged and pleaded for us to go on. We never begged so much for anything in our whole lives as we did then…to just go on. Our fear of being caught by the Russians was so great.

We must have stayed in this city for two days trying to figure out what direction we should go next. By this time, we didn't know what day it was, how long we had been on the road or how far away we were from home… nor did we care anymore. By the second day we were so hungry, but there wasn't any food to be found. Around noon some people told us that there was a butcher shop in town that was giving away all kinds of sausage. They were trying to get rid of it before the town was taken over by the enemy. It was better to give it away to the refugees than to let the Russians benefit from it. Mama took Harry and left immediately, determined to get some of it for us.

They were gone for such a long time that Opa and I began to worry. Mama, at the same time, was doing a lot of extra walking around town in the vain hope that maybe, just maybe, she would see Papa. Whenever she saw a man or a group of people, she would walk over and ask where they were from, hoping that one of them might have come from the area our Papa had been and have some news of him. She was told that in the area where Papa had been assigned there had been a lot of intense fighting.

As Opa, Herbert and I waited; the people around us began frantically running around and talking excitedly. We wondered what was happening. A man in the crowd said that there was a train coming through from the front line going west. He said this was the last train leaving the front line other than a train carrying wounded soldiers. This train was only going to take children, the elderly and the sick. No one else would be allowed to get on.

CHAPTER 5

THE TRAIN

Everyone around us started to leave for the train station and Mama and Harry had not returned. I dressed Herbert, got ourselves buttoned up and waited. Still no one came. I started to cry and so did Herbert, but Opa tried to cheer us up saying they would come real soon.

But they didn't and soon everyone around us was gone except for those who had someone in their family die. They were, then, reluctant to leave. We decided we'd better go so we could follow the crowds in order to find the train station. We walked for awhile. All of a sudden we heard our names. We looked down the street and saw Mama and Harry running towards us. They said they had heard about the train and knew everyone was leaving the school. As soon as they heard the news they immediately ran the long distance back to us but it had snowed a lot the day before and it was very difficult to walk through the deep drifts. We thanked God again for re-uniting us. Together we walked to the station. There were a lot of train tracks and masses of people coming from all directions, but… no train.

We stood close together because the people were pushing and shoving. No one knew which track the train was going to arrive on. After what seemed a very long time, we could see the train coming. We happened to be near the right track but on the wrong side. We reasoned that since the train had doors on both sides, we should be able to get on from where we stood. The people that stood at the wrong tracks rushed over. There was such a huge mob of people and they all knew it was their last chance to escape. The mad rush was terrible-people will do anything if they are desperate. It became a matter of life or death. It was awful to see what could happen when a mob panics.

The train was extremely long. It had 84 cars. Three of them were passenger cars and all the rest were boxcars. The people would not move out of the way for fear of losing their place in the front of the crowd. Many tried to cling to the train as it moved slowly into the station. People were run over and the train dragged many of them because they couldn't wait until it had stopped. The fear of being left behind was worse than anything else imaginable. I can remember so clearly a woman pushing her baby in a stroller. She was determined to get to the track the train was on. She hurried frantically to cross all the empty tracks, but the stroller kept getting caught in the deep snow and the tracks. She tried so desperately to make it, she crossed in the path of the on-coming train (as did many others). Mama turned us away so we wouldn't see the awful tragedy that befell this young mother and her child. I can remember the train didn't stop–it just kept coming until it was halfway through the station. People were screaming and running and crying all around it. It was a nightmare. In all our previous days we had seen many dead people...even many babies. But, here we saw the most gruesome deaths yet. Many lost their lives here.

When the train finally came to a stop, we ended up standing by a boxcar. We helped Mama and little Herbert get on first and then Opa. Other people got on at the same time, so Mama and Opa ended up in the middle of the group of people. This was good because it was a lot warmer in between the crowd. The floor was covered with straw. Harry and I got a little spot closer to the door, but we were all on board and that was all that mattered. It was dark before the train began moving out of the station. Someone had pushed the big door shut, but there were many cracks and holes where we could see out. However, through those same holes and cracks came the bitter cold. After sitting for a long time we felt the terrible hunger pains again. Before getting on the train, we had no time to feel the hunger. I can't remember if Mama got any sausage in that city. I cannot remember eating any. All I remember is feeling terribly cold and so hungry. Much later we learned that during this whole time since we left home the temperatures at night hovered between −20 to −30°C.[12]

All of the people were packed into the boxcar so tightly; there was no room to move even a muscle. Some tried singing, but it was so half-hearted and made all of us feel so sad, that it didn't work. Everyone was silently praying for the strength and resolve to go on.

I don't know how but we must have slept a little. It wasn't long before someone had to go to the toilet and soon more had to go. After searching around, someone found some kind of can and it was passed around. It was eventually passed to Harry or me because we were next to the door. Harry had to try and pour it out of a crack or a hole by the door, whichever worked the best. We were able to get rid of it and, so, another problem was solved.

After dozing some more we woke up to see daylight coming in through the cracks and someone said, "We're not moving!" And sure enough, we were at a standstill. There were tracks beside us but our train stood on an unused track in the middle of nowhere. According to the movement of the sun, we sat there for a very long time. One man said it was now afternoon and, still, the train just sat there. We felt as if we were left there to freeze to death. Everyone was getting colder and colder. Many were to the point of freezing to death and falling asleep. Hands and feet were becoming frostbitten. Many babies and elderly people died from the bitter cold. At this point, Harry saved my life by not allowing me to fall asleep and succumb to hypothermia. A man, also standing by the door, pushed it open a little and reached for some snow. He rubbed our hands and faces with it to restore our circulation. The only thing Mama could think about were the three heated passenger cars at the front of the train. It must have been on her mind all day, thinking about what she could do about it, because all of a sudden she said, "We are going to jump out and go to the front of the train and try to get into one of the passenger cars." Harry and I started to cry because we were afraid there wouldn't be any room and we would be left in the field. But Mama said, "We have to try it, because we will freeze to death here anyway. We have to do it." So we pushed the door open and looked out. There were open fields as far as we could see. Along the tracks was a ditch.

The ditch was full of snow and we thought it would be hard enough to walk on and not too high to jump over if we had to. After we jumped off the train, Mama jumped with Herb in her arms and, then, Opa. Opa was in such bad physical shape by now. He had to be forced every step of the way as he had no strength left to be able to do it on his own. We started walking towards the front of the train, trying to hurry as fast as we could. After we had gone a little way the snow became softer and we sank to our knees and even deeper in some places. We tried to get to a place where the snow wouldn't be so deep but ended up having to stay in the ditch because there was a fence right alongside it. We kept going when all of a sudden the train's whistle blew…once…twice…and we started crying and running. If the third whistle blew, that meant it was leaving. We fell in the deep snow and crawled on all fours, pushing and pulling Opa. Harry and I were screaming because we knew if we were left behind, we wouldn't have very long to live. Just when we reached the first passenger car the whistle blew again…once…twice…Mama had a difficult time reaching the door, it was so high up. The windows and the door were frosted and frozen and no matter how hard she tried, Mama could not get it open. She pounded and screamed in utter hysteria and finally it opened. We had been on the wrong side when we had gotten off the train and now the door, which opened, was piled high with boxes and other items. We could see someone moving through all of it and soon saw it was a soldier. He was a medic in the German army. He had heard our desperate screams and helped Mama open the door. All the boxes and other things fell out before we were able to get in. He helped us climb aboard and, once there, we wept from exhaustion and relief that, once again, we had made it.

When we looked around the car, we didn't know what to do. It was so crowded in there; you couldn't take a step in any direction. It felt so hot to us because we had been so very cold. The heat was foul and sickening from so many unwashed bodies all crammed together so tightly. The medic managed to move through the car somehow and looked into all the compartments trying to find a place for Mama and Opa. He finally removed two younger people from one compartment and Mama, with the baby, and Opa had a place to rest. Harry and I had to stand in the aisle, which wasn't so bad except we had to stand on one leg at a time because it was so crowded. There were people lying on the floor stacked on top of each other. We noticed a good-sized ledge on the side of the windows and Harry and I thought that would be a better place to stand.

By this time the train had started moving again. I don't know how long we stood on that ledge but I remember falling asleep standing on it and waking up in the morning on top of the stack of people on the floor. When we woke up we were grateful to see that the train was still moving. The train moved very slowly. It was pulling 84 cars filled to much more than capacity and I guess it just could not pull all that weight any faster. That morning the toilet situation was accomplished in a little bowl that was passed around and thrown out. However, with no food or drink this was not a frequent problem. I can't remember what Mama did with baby Herbert's bottom. She must have changed him sometime, somewhere with something. I can't recall ever seeing her change him. I asked her later and she said she used whatever she could find.

It was now the second day on the train and there had been nothing to eat. We were so hungry and had no idea where any food or drink would come from. Later that day we stopped in a smaller city and there was the Red Cross. We thanked God for them so many times!! They gave us food. Each person received a package of four sandwiches. I always wondered if they had enough for all the people, because there were so many starving refugees and not a lot of food.

The train stood still for quite some time in this town. Here Harry and I got out and walked almost to the end of the train and counted the cars. While walking we found an old bottle that we thought we could use for Herbert to drink out of. Mama still had the bag of sugar wrapped up next to Herb's little body inside that big old fur coat. It was a good place to keep it so it wouldn't get lost. Mama asked us to go outside and try to find some water. Since there was no milk, she would mix the water with a little of the sugar for Herbert. We went out but didn't know where to find water because everything was frozen. We walked past the train engines and saw hot water slowly running out from under the engine. We thought this was great. We held the bottle under there until it was full. It looked clean so we took it back to Mama. She was so happy to get it especially because it was hot. We told her where we had found it. She mixed it with the sugar and gave it to Herbert to drink. The poor little baby was so hungry. He was listless and slept most of the time. I do not remember ever hearing him cry. He was too weak. Opa slept a lot too and Mama said to let him sleep. "It was nearly as good as eating."

The train pulled out and we were relieved to be moving again. By this time we were in Pommern, a province toward the centre of Germany. Mama's cousin lived in Greifswalde by Stettin where Mama had taken all our summer clothing. That trip already seemed so long ago. She thought if we could just get that far then we could stay with her cousin. With summer coming, we would have some fresh clothing to wear. Other people must have had similar plans because some got off in little towns along the way to stay with relatives. Some left our compartment and we had a little more room. The baggage was gone, too, which meant the baggage carriers above us were empty so, when the train started to move again, Harry and I climbed up there and lay on them. This gave us a chance to get a good long sleep…and we slept a lot! I guess when you are starving you sleep a lot.

We woke up later in the night because there was a lot of noise and talking. We saw some people moving a long roll wrapped in a blanket. The men, one of whom was a medic, opened a window and threw out the rolled up blanket. We realized that it was a person who must have died through the night…and suddenly, we knew why, every morning, there was more room on the train. We wondered how many people had already been thrown out as we slept each night.

The medic went around and checked the refugees to make sure there were no dead people remaining on the train. Typhoid was a constant threat…if that became a reality there would be no hope for any of us. We were horrified when the medic came into our compartment and looked closely at Opa who looked lifeless slouched over in a corner on his side. The medic called in the other men with the blanket. Mama leapt to Opa's side and put her head to his chest and listened to see if he was breathing. We were hysterical and crying, too. Mama and the men were arguing. She would not let them take Opa. She said, "He's not dead yet, he is still breathing!" Mama talked so fast and cried so hard that finally the men left.

In the morning when we awoke, the train was standing still again on a lonely track in an open field. Someone came in and said the train engineer told them that a chicken farm near a town up ahead was giving away chickens to anyone who wanted one. Mama was so excited! We had to stay with Herb and Opa while she went to talk to the engineer. After a while she came back and said she was going to get some chickens. The engineer wanted some, too and since he couldn't leave the train, they made a deal. In case the train had to leave while she was gone, he would stop for Mama in this town and blow the whistle three times or he would leave without her. In return, Mama would bring chickens back for him, too. Mama left. Harry and I were terrified. We just sat there the whole time without saying a word. It seemed like it took hours, but she came back and there we still sat exactly as we were when she left. Then she made another deal with the engineer. He said he didn't know how long the train would have to sit there…it could be another hour…another day…or longer. He had orders to stay off the main track and couldn't leave until another train carrying wounded soldiers passed by heading west. The chickens were cleaned but raw and Mama said she would go to a farm across a nearby field and see if she could cook the chickens–his, too–but he was to give her a warning if he received orders to leave and enough time to get back to the train. He agreed and Mama left again. She crossed a field to a farm that must have been about two kilometres away. She had been gone quite awhile when the Red Cross train went by. It had big red crosses all over the sides and roofs of the train cars. This indicated that it was a train carrying wounded and so it would not be attacked. Everybody had to make room for it so it could hurry west.

After the train had gone it was silent again. The engineer blew the whistle three times. There came Mama running across the field. The chickens didn't get cooked too much but we did have some broth to drink and we managed to pull off some of the meat with our teeth. It was tough all right, but it was hot and it was something to put in our stomachs. Mama would only give us a little and the rest she kept for later. So that it wouldn't spoil, she opened the window, tied the chickens to the window handle and hung them outside. We felt a little better after eating some food.

The next day the train stopped again in another town and the Red Cross was there with chicken broth and sandwiches. Only people who had a container could get some broth. The other people in our compartment asked Harry and me if we could get some for them and we did. They gave us the container that had been used for bathroom purposes. Since we were smaller, we could work our way through the crowds faster to get to the Red Cross truck and were able to bring back some broth for other people, too. Quite a few people were able to get a good hot drink of broth with their sandwich.

Things seemed a little brighter now…except that Opa looked so ill. He was still sleeping and wouldn't eat any food. Outside it was getting warmer now and there was only a little snow left on the ground. On the other side of the tracks there was a little pond and there wasn't any ice on it. Harry and I walked over and washed our faces and hands a little bit, but it was too cold for that. Can you imagine? We never had our clothing off nor had anything on us washed since we left our farm. That seemed like an eternity ago. I know we must have been filthy and stinking. Starvation, also, creates a terrible odour…how well we learned that!

Mama thought that if we travelled all night, sometime the next day we should arrive at her cousin's place. The next day, in the afternoon, we were there but, we didn't get off the train. Everyone told us we were crazy to consider getting off because the Russians were quite close behind us and we would have to flee again in a couple days. So, we thought we better stay on and go as far as the train would take us. Mama said we had a distant aunt in Luebeck, Holstein, and that we probably could go there. But, surely we wouldn't have to go that far west! The Russians couldn't possibly get *that* far into Germany! At least, that was what we had heard someone say. The Oder River was in front of us and surely that was as far as the Russian army would advance. Our train was the last one to cross the Oder River.

CHAPTER 6
GUESTROW, MECKLENBURG

I think the train travelled, with frequent stops, for two more days after that. It travelled steadily towards Guestrow, Mecklenburg and there it stopped. Because so many refugees had perished, only half of the original boxcars and "passengers" were still on the train compared to when we left Preussisch-Stargard. In Guestrow, the Red Cross was waiting to assist the refugees getting off the train…helping them find a place to sleep, food to eat and help for the ill. They helped the injured and sick first and one of those was my Opa. Mama asked the Red Cross agent if there was any kind of special care available for him. Two Red Cross workers put Opa in a little wagon and pulled him to a nursing home. We all wept tears of sadness but knew this was the only way we could help him. They, then, directed us to a building that looked like it once might have been a school. Once we were there, the Red Cross ushered us into a separate room to remove the lice we had in our hair and clothes. They took our clothing away to be fumigated and treated our heads with medicine. They had big tanks for us to have a bath. Mama cried bitterly after undressing Herbert and seeing how thin and emaciated he had become. Herb had beautiful shoulder length blonde hair, wavy and curly. Now, it was all matted and dirty. It had to be cut short to get rid of all the matted tangles. It was so sad! And he looked even thinner after his hair was shorn off. The Red Cross gave us different clothing to wear and some broth and bread for us to eat. After we were dressed and had left the fumigation room we saw that all of the floors in the schoolhouse were thickly covered with straw. The school was packed with refugees but we were able to claim a spot that we called our little home. We must have lain in that school for about three days although I can't remember how long it really was. It must have been around the middle of February now…a whole month since we left our home…a lifetime.

Arrangements had been made with the people that lived in and around this town to give up rooms for refugees coming from the east. Each family was allowed two rooms for themselves and the rest had to be donated for displaced persons to use. We got to stay with an older couple, Herr and Frau Schlichting, who lived in a town a few kilometres away called Neu Wokern (east of Guestrow). Before we left, Mama went to see Opa in the nursing home. She was so pleased to see how much some tender loving care had helped him. Opa was well enough now that he could open his eyes, talk to Mama and understand what she was saying. She told him that we were going to live with some people in a nearby town and that she would come to see him whenever she could.

We rode a train to the Schlichting's home. They owned a grocery store, which had been closed for years. We were able to live in the "store" part of their home. We had a bed, table and lots of shelves. This was going to be our home. The people were very nice and, at the beginning, shared the little food they had with us. After that we had to find our own food.

In the days that followed, we tried to get cleaned up and regain a little of our strength. To get food, we went begging. We just walked door to door asking for something to eat or something to wear. It was amazing how the people, who had so little themselves, *did* share. Sometimes we would take baby Herbert along and people would give us things for him. We got some clothing and food, although only enough food for one day at a time. Mama was satisfied with that. She always said, "Fur Morgen wird Gott Sorgen," which means, "God will take care of tomorrow." He always did.

One day when we were begging (baby Herbert was with us), a family gave us a really nice stroller for Herbert. Mama shed tears of happiness for now she wouldn't have to carry Herb anymore. People gave us food that day which we could take home and cook, too. The old couple let us use their kitchen. The mayor of this town, also, distributed some food for the homeless. No one had any money, not even a single penny…absolutely nothing! Even if, by chance, someone had some money there was nothing for sale anywhere anyway. We were totally dependent on God and the common sense He gave us to do something about our situation as best we could.

The following week, Mama thought she should look into finding a church. We were finished fleeing now and, if this was to be our home, she wanted Harry and I to be confirmed. Since we had already gone to Confirmation classes for two years, she thought we could join a class here. The church she found was in a neighboring town called Klaber and they were holding a Confirmation service on the 18th of March. The pastor said if Harry and I would come twice a week to classes we could get confirmed along with the rest of the group. Frau Schlichting knew I didn't have a proper dress for my Confirmation, so she made one for me from a dress that had belonged to her daughter. It was brown with a white collar. She was so kind and I was so thankful! It reminded me, though, of my beautiful black velveteen dress with rhinestones that was left behind on our wagon. Mama had it made for my Confirmation back home in Peterkau… I felt such sadness.

CHAPTER 7

CONFIRMATION

Our Confirmation day was bittersweet. Schlichtings had some friends who let us use their horse and wagon to get to church. The weather was dreary and rainy that day. The roads were very muddy. We were so thankful we didn't have to walk. We got to church and it was full of people. The class walked up to the front in pairs. Harry and I walked together. As the Confirmands knelt, the Pastor placed his hand on our heads to bless us. At each child's turn, the family members stood up. When it was our turn, Mama stood up all alone and we could hear her crying. We couldn't help it and we started to cry, too. When the Confirmation rites were finished, we had to stand while the Confirmation hymn was sung, "O' take my hand, dear Father, and lead Thou me, 'Til at my journey's ending, I dwell with Thee. Alone, I cannot wander, one single day. So do Thou guide my footsteps, on life's rough way."[13] Hearing these words shattered our already fragile hearts and we wept bitterly. How true the words were! What anguish and pain we felt! If only our dear Papa could have been there with us. Where was he? Was he alive? Was he hurt? Please God lead him to us, we prayed silently in our hearts.

After it was over, the minister announced that everyone going home to a festive meal should, please, remember those without anything to eat. If they could share, they were to stop and see him before going home. We got our Confirmation certificates and climbed back into our mud-splattered wagon and went home, too. When we got back to the storeroom, the Schlichtings had made some pea soup for us and had the table set so nicely! What a surprise! They had kept little Herb for us, too, while we went to church. It was the best pea soup any of us had ever eaten. No one really said too much, but we certainly experienced mixed feelings that day in our hearts. Suddenly there was knocking at the door and children from the church came in with food. They brought bowls filled with many different kinds of hot food. It was so wonderful and so nice of them! We were so happy and thankful, we wept tears of joy. There never seemed to be an end to all the weeping we did that day…one wonders where all the tears came from.

CHAPTER 8
SURVIVING IN MECKLENBURG

The next time Mama went to see Opa, he was feeling much better and was beginning to get up a little more each day. Mama felt better knowing he was being cared for and was getting stronger.

Then, Mama looked into the matter of schooling. But because of the war and no available teachers the schools were all closed. Mama thought I should go into home economics. I was hired by a licensed farm family as an apprentice. (I was still only thirteen years old!) They lived in Gross Wokern, four kilometres from Schlichtings. The wages were paltry, but I received free room and board and I could eat here without having to stop before I was full. I shared my room with another apprentice named Elfriede. She was nice, but was a local girl from that area so she could not relate to how I felt or what we'd lost. In spite of that, we became quite good friends.

We had to work hard. We were up in the morning at six o'clock, made a fire in the stove and prepared breakfast for a large group of men who worked on the farm. They *always* ate the same thing for breakfast: fried potatoes and milk soup with buttered bread. Oh, but it tasted so good! I must have eaten like a man! It was quite often, too, that a lonely man would come to the door and beg for a piece of bread. They always were given something to eat, or if we were ready to eat a meal, he was invited to join us at the table. I would always watch out for these men, hoping that one of them might be Papa. But they were always somebody else's Papa who was looking for his family.

Frau Bartel was the lady of the house. She was very mean and unfriendly. She would always yell at us. We did all of the cleaning and it was a very large house. The kitchen floor was made of red brick and every time we were finished with the dishes we had to wash the floor, too. We found it easier to wash it on our hands and knees, but she would come along and kick us and shout, "What's the matter? Don't your backs bend?" We were never allowed to kneel on any job, only to bend down. When cleaning the carpet in their private quarters (there were no vacuum cleaners then) we had to bend over and brush the whole carpet with a hand brush and dustpan. Elfriede and I were so happy when evening came and we could go to our room. But, the misery was somewhat worth it for the food we got, if nothing else. We never had any trouble sleeping either! But, I was *so* homesick for Mama, Harry and Herb. After all, I was only thirteen years old and Elfriede was just one year older. I cried myself to sleep in my pillow almost every night.

Some evenings we would dress really warm and walk home. Elfriede would walk with me so I wouldn't have to go alone. We picked clear nights when there was a moon so we could see our way. Believe me, we were so scared! With all kinds of enemy people and war prisoners around, no one was safe. But, I just had to get home to see Mama, so once in awhile we would do it.

The country road we walked on was outlined with trees on each side. One night we were walking back after a visit home. It was very still, deserted and quiet. Elfriede and I were talking together in whispers when, suddenly, we heard a plane pass overhead. It turned around and zoomed back lower over our heads. Then, it turned once more and we heard the roar of the engines as it swooped down towards us again. I knew by the sound that we were in terrible trouble. We ran into a shaded part of the field and lay in a deep furrow. The plane came swooping down, very low beside the trees, and strafed the ground all along the trees with machine guns. We lay with our faces in the dirt and our hands folded, praying and believing that God would not let us die. The plane left. But, even after the plane disappeared and it was quiet and still once again, we lay there not moving for a long time. Finally, we got up and ran in the shadows of the trees, moving from tree to tree, our hearts pounding, until we reached the farm. This was one night we wished the moon hadn't been so bright.

I worked for another week and when Mama heard about our terrifying ordeal with the bomber and the conditions at the farm, she made me return home. She said she'd rather we go hungry together, then have one of us go through something like that again.

Life got a little better. We always had some kind of food to eat. It continued to get warmer outside. We still begged for food and we would go walking to see what we might find that would be edible. When we did discover something we would pick it up and take it home for Mama to cook. One time Harry and I were walking alongside some railway tracks where some train cars were sitting. There we found a beet lying on the ground. We kept walking and saw another one and, then, another. We picked them up wondering where they came from. We looked up and saw boxcars piled full of beets. Some had fallen off. Harry lifted me up onto the boxcar and I threw some down. Harry put them inside his coat. I jumped off, took some, too, and we ran home to Mama. She was so happy and she made several meals from them. When we told her how we got them, she told us it would be all right and God would forgive us as long as we took *only* what we needed to survive and no more.

After we had eaten all the beets, Mama told us to go back and get some more. But, this time, the boxcars filled with beets were gone and in their place stood cars filled with briquettes. We took some of those and, again, Mama was happy because now we had something with which to make a fire.

One day Harry went with Mama to see Opa while I stayed behind to care for Herb. On their way to Guestrow their train was attacked by British warplanes. They said it was absolutely terrible. There was an ammunition factory, halfway to Guestrow, hidden in the woods. The train stopped there when it was attacked. The planes were dropping napalm which is a gooey-sticky mass and when it landed and reached a certain temperature, it would catch fire. For example, if a little bit splashed on your skin, the warmth of your body caused it to ignite.

Somehow Harry and Mama escaped from all this horror and got back home. Another week had gone by when we heard that the Russians were still advancing and that they weren't very far away. The area homeowners couldn't believe that they were now facing what we were faced with several months before. All the roads were becoming clogged with refugees once again. Farmers were preparing wagons to flee just as we had done. Suddenly, that sickening, frightening feeling descended upon us once again.

Mama quickly boarded the train to Guestrow and got Opa. We thought if anything happens Opa should be with us. Mama returned in the evening with Opa. We were all *so* happy to see him! He walked well and acted and looked like he used to. It was a happy re-union.

CHAPTER 9
RETURN TO THE TRECK

The Russians were fighting by Berlin, only about one hundred kilometres from where we were. The mayor made an announcement saying that if people decided to flee, they were on their own. He said they must pick their own time and their own destination. That evening Mama put us to bed early so we would get a good night's sleep because no one knew what the next day would bring. By morning we could hear the rumbling of cannon fire and we prepared to leave. We hoped to be gone by 3:00 p.m. because we didn't want to make the same mistake we made last time by leaving too late. We took Herb's stroller and loaded it full of the few belongings we had plus some food. This time the stroller was our getaway vehicle. We took turns pushing it, carrying Herbert and hanging onto Opa. Sometimes we sat Herb on top of the stroller and gave him short rides. We walked through Gross Wokern and then onto a path through a field. Many others were doing the same thing.

It was April 29th when we left. I don't think I will ever forget that day. It was Papa's birthday and over four months since the last time we saw him. We kept walking and walking all night until morning when we arrived in Krywitz, Mecklenburg. Mama became exhausted quickly this time. The grief and worry about the unknown were taking its toll again. We stayed with a very nice family here who had decided not to flee. They were very kind. Mama was so exhausted and said that she didn't think we'd go on any further. She said we couldn't walk anymore with a toddler and an old man. Harry left to go scouting around the neighbourhood. The German Army was everywhere now. They weren't fighting anymore; they just wanted to go west and save themselves like the rest of us. A German lieutenant saw Harry and asked him if he would like to trade coats so he could cover up his uniform. At first, Harry thought this was great but quickly realized that this was not a wise decision and quickly got rid of the coat. Later that day, the lieutenant came back with Harry and asked if he could join us and make believe he was a part of our family. Because of him, we were, then, able to get a ride on an army truck going west.

Again we found ourselves riding in the back of a truck only this time, because it was almost May, it wasn't so cold. When we got to the highway we found the same situation we found when we left our home. The highway was not wide. It was supposed to be a two-lane highway for two-way traffic. But both lanes were jammed full of refugees all going in the same direction…West. On the right side there were families in their wagons loaded with their belongings and on the left side was the army. It was "bumper-to-bumper" but moving steadily. This time it was a double treck…civilians *and* military.

In the afternoon, the lieutenant got word on his radio to watch for enemy planes. They had spotted fighter-jets coming our way. He sat hanging out of the window, with field glasses, watching the sky. Suddenly he spotted them and shouted. The truck stopped abruptly and everyone had to get out. (We had picked up a whole truckload of people by now.) But the people just sat there dumbfounded, in disbelief and shock, just looking around. In a flash the bombers were over us, they came so fast! They circled a couple of times, very low, and we could see the American markings. We now knew, for sure, they were enemy planes. However, they didn't attack. They made another circle and flew away. It seemed too good to be true. We all got back on the truck and started driving again, but the lieutenant said they would return and when they did and he yelled, he wanted everyone to MOVE! And do it FAST! Next time they will attack!

We didn't get very far, perhaps only a kilometre or so when he spotted them again. The truck screeched to a halt and he screamed, "OUT! EVERYBODY MO-O-O-O-VE!" I tell you, everybody moved! People jumped, got pushed or were thrown off. People were running frantically everywhere. People, from the wagons and the army trucks, jumped over the steep ditch embankment not far from the road. They headed towards a small patch of woods a short distance from the road. Everyone tried to get there as fast as possible. I remember how Harry and I jumped off that truck and Harry ran for the woods. Mama threw Herb into my arms and I took off running. How Mama got Opa off that truck, I don't know, but I do know that I stumbled at the top of that embankment and Herb and I rolled down into the ditch.

By this time the bombers were zooming over us peppering us with bullets. I picked up Herb and screamed hysterically. His whole face was covered with blood and he was shrieking at the top of his lungs. People were yelling, "Run for the trees!" I ran to the woods and crouched low to the ground with Herb pressed against my chest. Mama and Opa were all ready there. Mama grabbed Herb, praying and sobbing because she believed a bullet had hit him. The planes had seen people run for the woods and they continually swooped over the trees, spraying them with machine gun fire. They circled over and over continually attacking it and the area. Mama made us all huddle close together and she put her arms around us. She said that if we were hit she wanted them to hit us all…she didn't want one of us to be left all alone.

We huddled together praying and crying while bullets sprayed all around us. Finally the attacks ended and it was still. There was not a single sound. Harry left our huddle to see if he could find a medic or someone to help little Herbert. He returned with a medic who examined Herb and discovered that he had a big gash inside his mouth, which he must have received when we tumbled down the embankment. The medic stopped the bleeding and gave Mama something to press against it.

Our attention was directed once again to what was going on around us. There was a lot of yelling and soldiers were running everywhere. Wagons and trucks were on fire and many people had been wounded or killed. Little clusters of people were weeping, huddled over the body of a loved one. The lieutenant from our truck kept shouting out orders for the people to keep moving and hurry back to the trucks. He said that whoever wanted a ride had better come quickly because he was leaving *right now*! Not far ahead was a truck loaded with 'panzerfaust' (grenades). This vehicle had been hit in the attack and was on fire. It could explode any second! We quickly climbed back on the same truck we were on earlier. But, now the driver hesitated, not knowing if he should drive towards the impending explosion. He knew if it exploded when we were near it, we would all be blown up along with it. But if we waited, we could be delayed enough that the Russians would catch up to us. The other option would be to attempt it on foot. He decided to risk it. There was just enough room for us to pass. He put the truck in gear and started to move ahead.

At that moment, we realized that Harry was not in the truck. We looked around crying and screaming for the driver to stop. He wouldn't stop. If he did it could mean that we could all be killed if the burning munitions truck exploded. We couldn't see Harry anywhere. Then we saw a large group of people in the field running away from the road. They were running in a big arc around the burning truck. Someone must have told them about the explosives. They were all people who had family members on our truck and in that group we saw Harry.

The truck drove as fast as it could. We all closed our eyes and huddled together on the floor, as it was impossible to stand because it was so rough. The truck hit rocks, trees and branches in our great haste to get around that truck and far enough away from it before it exploded. We made it! And, oh, the relief that soared through all of us! Everyone shouted with joy and praised the driver and lieutenant for making their decision. The truck stopped to wait for the people who belonged with us including Harry. We looked around to see the catastrophe behind us. It was a sight from hell. Indescribable. Horrific. Many wagons on the civilian side were on fire. Horses, still in their harnesses, had been shot or one was shot and the other still standing quivering in fear. There were cows tied behind wagons and they were shot dead or wounded, still hanging by their ropes connected to the wagons. Many bodies were hanging out of wagons. We saw one wagon where both horses had been shot and the entire family was killed except for one little girl who was sitting in the midst of it all weeping bitterly. She was blond and, perhaps, about four or five years old. The lieutenant jumped out of our truck, ran back, picked her up and took her with him into the cab of the truck. We didn't stop long...we had to get going because another report came through the radio of more bombers coming.

We drove very fast, desperately trying to get as far away as fast as we could. It seemed like we were the only ones left to be able to leave that horrifying scene. Nobody had any time to think about what had just happened. No chance to absorb it. What becomes of all the people and animals that lay there dead? No one knew anyone's names. But these thoughts didn't linger long at that moment. We were desperate to save ourselves.

Suddenly we heard the planes coming again. The driver turned off the main highway onto a side road into the country. This road was lined on both sides with thick groves of trees. He drove as fast as the truck would go right into a clump of trees and stopped it right under them. From our sheltered spot we could watch this second attack on the vehicles and refugees left on the highway. We were numb. It all seemed like a nightmare! So senseless! So brutal!

After the planes left once again, we continued driving down that dirt road until we came to a town. It must have rained the day before because there was water standing on the road and the truck slid all over. We noticed a single plane overhead and prayed it wouldn't spot us. When we arrived in the town of Plate, it seemed quiet and, relatively, peaceful. We saw a few army trucks and wagons standing around. When we stopped, the soldiers told us to find shelter because we would probably be staying here awhile. They said it was not safe to go out on the highway now. They were all tired of the war and wanted to stay until the British or American forces arrived, if possible. They were hoping and praying that they would be a little friendlier than the ones in the air. The driver left us in the village and the lieutenant stayed with us as a family member.

Night was coming and that was in our favour. It was now the 30th of April. We went to the mayor and he took us to a school where straw had been spread on the floor. Some refugees were already there but it wasn't crowded. The Red Cross supplied us with something to eat. We received instructions to lie under a window and not walk around. Because of the angle, there was less chance of getting hit by enemy fire when lying under the window. Planes were still circling the town and shooting could still be heard from the highways. We had to constantly be prepared for the possibility of a direct attack. The fighting continued all around Plate all through the night and we could hear it very well. We slept sporadically that night. The next day, we spent a lot of time lying down under cover and only getting up, with great care and caution, to get food from the Red Cross. Another night was soon upon us. We were filled with fear and worry.

CHAPTER 10
THE WAR IS OVER!

The next morning, May 2nd, we awoke to see the enemy walking the streets…the British army. Everything was, suddenly, so quiet. We couldn't believe it. And of course, we were scared. You can't imagine how frightened we were. It was terrifying not knowing what was going to happen next. Our goal was to get to Luebeck, Holstein, to Tante Mitze. But would we be able to get there now?

Mama finally mustered up enough courage to go outside. She could speak some English and thought she could get some information from a British soldier who was standing outside. He was surprised that Mama could speak English. He told her that they were there for only a few days and the Russians were going to take over that part of the country. Germany would be divided into sectors according to Eisenhower's command after the official surrender. Mama asked him if he would let us know when that time came, because after all this hardship and coming this far, we certainly didn't want to end up in a sector under Communist rule.

Now we were able to walk around freely. Mama went to the mayor's office where the Red Cross had set up a committee to help the homeless. They passed out food stamps and some money. Mama got some stamps and 200 RM.[14] Now we could buy something if we could only find a store with groceries in it! We looked around to see what had happened to the German army. We did not see a single German soldier. The German lieutenant, who was still with us, left, dressed in civilian clothing, to go home to his family. We had heard that all German soldiers had to report as prisoners-of-war to receive a military discharge. The little girl he had rescued was turned over to the Red Cross.

On May 5th, Mama was outside and saw the teacher from the school take down the German flag. Mama asked what it means and he said, "The war is over. Hitler is dead." Mama came into the school and told everyone there what she had heard. Some, like us, were happy but some wouldn't believe it. They kept saying, "Germany won't lose this war." It was unbelievable that there were some that still believed in victory...even when things were so bad!

We had to make plans as to where we should go, what direction and how we should travel. Mama had passed on the British soldier's information about the Russians' imminent arrival. Most of the refugees wanted to move on, except, of course, for the people who lived in that town. Almost all of the townspeople stayed. There was one wealthy landlord from the treck, who owned several wagons, but had no drivers left. He asked if Opa would drive a wagon for him. If so, he would allow Mama and the baby to ride, too. But, Harry and I would have to walk. Of course, we didn't care, as long as there was a way to leave. Mama accepted the offer and told him she would inform him when we got word from the British to leave.

That night, at two in the morning, there was a knock at the school window. Mama went out and was told that the Russians were to arrive by morning and the British would move out at that time. Everything moved really fast then. By now we had learned to be ready to jump and go at any time. While Mama got Herbert ready, she told Harry to hurry to the landlord and tell him it was time to go. When we got there, we quickly helped him hitch up the horses. Mama and Opa climbed into the wagon with Herbert and away we went. Harry and I hung on to the back of the wagon just to make sure we wouldn't get lost. There were many others, too, that had to walk and they, also, held onto their wagons. It was a lot easier walking if you were pulled along.

We moved along quickly and in the beginning, some of the time, we even had to run. After a few days rest, the horses were ready to run, too, so we made good headway. It was now the 6th of May and Harry and I walked or ran all day. The landlord gave us a sandwich...I wonder where they got it from? It was so delicious, especially since it was all we ate that day. We took only dirt roads, avoiding main highways. I remember the weather was so beautiful this day. It was a warm, sunny spring day. The trees were getting greener and the sweet smelling grass was green and fresh. Harry and I took our shoes off and went barefoot until Mama saw us and made us put our shoes back on.

We drove alongside some woods, going much slower because the horses were tired. Harry and I would walk ahead some of the time. We got to a place in the woods where there was a little meadow. It was pretty so Harry and I walked off to the side to see it better when we saw an abandoned horse. And such a beautiful horse it was! I had never seen one as beautiful as that one! No one was around–just the horse with a halter and a rope dangling down. It was contentedly grazing. We went close to the horse and examined it. Then we ran back to the wagon and asked Mama if I could have it. Mama told me I shouldn't because it might be wild and I might get hurt. Besides, she said I wouldn't be able to catch it anyway. "But, if I catch it can I keep it?" I asked her. She said I could. I quickly ran back to the horse. I just loved horses and I wanted it so badly. Harry kept saying, "He's going to run away!" But, I edged closer and closer, very slowly, talking constantly to him. He raised his head to look at me and I stretched out my hand and he smelled it. I scratched his head and slowly reached for the rope and—he was mine! I was ecstatic! I had a horse! I had nothing else in this world, but I had a horse! I couldn't believe it. I led him to the wagons and everyone looked him over. They thought he was a runaway or someone might have left him loose. They didn't think he was a working horse because there was no trace of harness marks. I didn't care about the 'whys' or 'hows'…I had a horse! And from then on wherever I went, that horse went, too.

CHAPTER 11
POGRESS, MECKLENBURG

At the end of the day we knew we'd have to stop and rest. We drove into a village called Pogress that was in Mecklenburg. Many British soldiers occupied it. Mama talked to some of them and they were happy to meet someone who could speak both languages. Mama helped translate for them. We stayed in Pogress for awhile. We found straw to use for bedding and slept in a barn. Then, some people took us in although we had to sleep on their living room floor. They were farm labourers and had small living quarters…but, they were so kind and even though they didn't have much to eat they shared whatever they had with us. These people were naturalized German citizens who had stayed in Germany after World War I. They had been our age at the time of the first world war and their folks did not want to return to Russia after the war since they were born Ukrainians. They could understand what we had experienced. I tied my horse outside onto a fence where there was a lot of grass. The people said we could stay with them until we could make a life for ourselves or find a home.

We thought we could finally stop now that the British army was in possession of the area…this was as far as we wanted to go. It was a blessing to know we didn't have to run anymore.

The British soldiers were nice to all of us. They handed out chocolate bars to all the little children. It was the first time most of the children had ever tasted chocolate. It was fun to watch a Jeep drive into the village and a dozen children rush to meet it. If it didn't stop, they would run after it until it did. One day an official from the British army wanted to talk with the mayor of the town. They asked Mama if she would be a translator. The British wanted to pay her but she didn't want any money, just food. So they brought us cans of meat and dry goods and SOAP, which we really needed! We shared our food with the Ukrainian couple. We always cooked everything together with them. Every day I took my horse alongside the roads to eat grass. I wanted to ride him so badly, but since I didn't have a bridle, I was afraid to. It's hard to handle a horse with just a halter. If you are just leading the horse then the halter works fine.

Mama didn't really like me to have the horse. She was worried that if we wanted to go somewhere else or find a place of our own to live, the horse would be inconvenient. One day a farmer was talking to Mama and asked her about our horse. She was glad that he wanted to buy it. However, she told him that it was my horse and he would have to ask me about it. I did not want to give him up but, I could see Mama's point and agreed to sell him. We got a bag of flour, two feather pillows and a large side of bacon for him. I knew I wouldn't be able to keep him for long anyway. Later, I walked down the road, sat behind a hedge and watched the horse on the farm where he now lived. The farmer had a difficult time with him because he had never been harnessed before. He wouldn't work in a team and when he was supposed to pull, he'd turn around all the time. The farmer would hit him and I wished I could go and take him away. I went to Mama crying and she told me I shouldn't go back there and watch him anymore. And so, reluctantly, with a broken heart, I didn't.

A week or so later, we found shelter for ourselves in an old fire station. We slept on straw on the floor again. We used boxes for a table and cooked some of our food at the Ukrainian couple's house. Bacon was the most valuable food and Mama would ration it out every day for one of our meals. We would get a small hunk of raw smoked bacon, the size of two fingers, and a piece of sourdough bread. Of course, we would always want the bacon to be the size of our two middle fingers! We would each get a knife and we would cut the piece of bacon, lay it on the bread and pop it into our mouth. It was *so-o-o-o-o* good!

The war was now officially over and it was supposed to be peacetime. But, now, what were we supposed to do? Tante[15] Mitze was our only relative in Luebeck. It had been our goal to end our journey there. Mama and our relatives from West Prussia had agreed that this would be the place where we could all find or contact each other. Because the fire station was not being used, the Burgermeister allowed us to live there temporarily. Mama kept translating for the British troops whenever she was needed and they paid her with food. One day, after we had been there a couple of weeks, an officer told Mama if it was possible for her to go further west, she should try to do so. The Russians and Americans were in a disagreement about where the sector boundary should go in that area. Again, for the second time, the British agreed to give up part of Germany to the Russians and the Americans would gain the south. This would, apparently, straighten out the boundary line. No one knew when this was to take place but it did mean that this place we were at would become part of the Russian sector. Mama thought hard about what we should do. We had no place to go and no more rides. There wasn't anyone on the roads anymore. Mama kept saying that Harry and I should go to Luebeck to Tante Mitze and stay there. But, after coming this far, we didn't think we should separate. Opa became ill again and was not able to go on foot. Harry wanted to go. He said that if we went to Tante Mitze's we could get some help. Luebeck was eighty kilometres away…how could they help us, if we *did* get there? I wanted to go, too, so he wouldn't be going alone.

CHAPTER 12
LUEBECK

When the time came for us to go, Mama got very worried and scared and said we shouldn't go. There were just too many things that could happen to us. We convinced her that we would do just fine. The Ukrainian couple told us to go in the direction of Zarrentin and then north to Ratzeburg and Luebeck. Mama showed us the path and said to watch the road signs and the sun for directions. She packed a few sandwiches for us and early one morning, at daybreak, we left. Mama's last instructions were, "Be careful…always remember your Confirmation song and remember to pray."

As we walked down the road we looked back and there stood Mama, still watching and waving her hand. I was glad when we went around a bend in the path and the hedges blocked our view of her. It was so sad seeing her standing there. I almost changed my mind and ran back.

It was now the third week of May and it was a beautiful day. The sun had risen so bright and beautiful that morning. We hadn't walked very far when we thought we were hungry enough to eat a little. It was sort of fun, just the two of us, on a mission. We felt important. Harry watched the road signs and I followed him. We came to the highway and walked and walked and walked. At one point we got thirsty and stopped at a farm to get something to drink. There was a huge, mean dog loose so we ran back to the highway. After awhile, we tried again and we met some friendly people. They said there was a well in the yard and we could help ourselves.

And we did! First Harry pumped and I cupped my hands and drank and then I pumped and Harry drank. It tasted so good! We were so thirsty and we drank a lot so we wouldn't have to stop again. In the early afternoon we ate the rest of our bread and kept walking. I was a little scared and kept asking Harry what we were going to do when it got dark. He kept saying, "Wait until it gets dark and then we'll think of something." We knew it would take us about three more days to reach Luebeck.

We rested for awhile and sat in the ditch thinking about what we should do. Evening was rapidly turning into night and suddenly Harry said, "I know; we'll try to stop somebody." I said, "You can't do that because the only vehicles on the road belong to the British or Canadian army and they wouldn't stop to pick us up." He said it wouldn't hurt to try.

We started walking again. Harry waved at everyone that went by, but there weren't many vehicles that passed us, just a Jeep here and there and none would stop. Harry probably would have done better without me because I was so scared I just hung onto his arm the whole time and wouldn't let go. Finally a car came and Harry stepped onto the road a little further and waved frantically until the car stopped. A man in civilian clothes asked what we were doing there. Harry told him that we were on our way to our aunt's house to get help because we left our mother, frail Opa and baby brother behind in Pogress. He couldn't believe we had walked all that way in one day. He asked us where our aunt lived. Harry, remembering a road sign he'd seen a little ways back that said *Ratzeburg 21 km,* answered, " She lives in Ratzeburg, Gneisenauerstrasse 49." "Well," this man said, "Why don't you get in the car and I'll drive you there. But first, we'll stop at my house in Seedorf for supper. Ratzeburg isn't that far away." This is what Harry had hoped for and that's why he'd said Ratzeburg instead of Luebeck. But, Harry was also hoping that he would just drop us off to find the street ourselves, since he had given the correct address but had lied about the city.

We talked a lot while we drove and he asked us a lot of questions. Harry told him a lot. He told him about all our experiences and even when our parents had come from Canada and how our Papa was lost in the war. This man was so astonished that we had to suffer so much in this country when we weren't German but Canadian citizens. He worked in Zarentin for the British embassy as an interpreter.

We stopped at his home in Seedorf and his warm and friendly wife gave us supper. After supper he took us to Ratzeburg and tried to find Gneisenauerstrasse 49. But, of course, he couldn't find it and no matter whom he asked they hadn't heard of it. Harry kept saying, "Just let us off and we'll find it." He wasn't about to leave us in the street all alone. Besides, it was past curfew, which meant all civilians had to be off the streets after 6:00 p.m. So he just kept on looking and, finally, one man said he had heard of such an address in Luebeck. I kept on poking Harry to say something and finally he did. He said, "Let's see that paper again that Mama gave us and see what it says...mmm...oh, yes...it does say Luebeck. I don't know what made me think it was Ratzeburg." "Oh well," our new friend said, "You were probably too tired to have noticed. I'll take care of both of you."

He drove into a big yard. All the buildings and trucks had big red crosses on them and we knew he had taken us to the Red Cross headquarters. He took us inside, gave his name and asked for the person in charge. He said, "I found these two kids on the road. They are Canadians and want to go to their aunt in Luebeck." It was hard to say good-bye to this man. He had been so kind and wanted the best for us. We were treated like royalty that night. We got to take a hot bath in a tub which was our first tub bath in our whole lives. We also got to sleep in a real bed. In the morning we had a good breakfast and the Red Cross took us to Luebeck in one of the Red Cross wagons. The driver was dressed all in white and he knew exactly where to go. He took us to the correct street and delivered us right to the door of Tante Mitze's house.

We rang the doorbell and Tante Mitze opened the door. At first she didn't know us, as it had been several years since she last saw us. After we told her who we were she opened her arms and hugged and kissed us. She pulled us inside and wanted to know where Mama, Papa, Opa and Herbert were. When we told her our story, she was so glad we had come to her. She said, "At first, I thought the rest were dead, since the two of you had come alone." Tante Lotte and Walter were there, too. They had come from West Prussia, also, almost from the same place where we had lived. Their farm had been only thirty kilometres from ours. They made it all the way with their wagons.

Onkel[16] Wilhelm wasn't with Tante Lotte and his son, Walter. Tante Lotte and Walter had brought along a good and faithful Italian prisoner-of-war who had worked for them when Onkel Wilhelm had to go to the army. Walter was sixteen years old and they didn't have any babies or old people to burden them on their flight to safety. We found out they had left two days earlier than we had and that is why they made it through with their wagons and belongings. They travelled steadily, sometimes all night, and made it the whole nine hundred and fifty kilometres to Tante Mitze's in plenty of time to avoid the Russians. Tante Lotte and Tante Mitze were sisters and Onkel Wilhelm and Mama were brother and sister. Tante Lotte didn't know where Onkel Wilhelm was. She never heard from him again and had no idea if he was alive or not. They had made it through with two wagons—two huge Belgian horses pulled the big one and one horse pulled the lighter one. This smaller horse, named Iwan, was a Russian horse from Siberia. They are small but are very strong. They had acquired him from a soldier who had brought him back from one of the Russian battlefronts. So, Tante Lotte was able to bring all their belongings with them. Since they got to Tante Mitze's they lent the horses out to a farmer in return for their feed and care. There was a shortage of horses and the farmer was happy to be able to use them.

When we finished telling our story and ending with Mama, Opa and Herbert waiting in Pogress and the news that the Russians were soon to take control of that area, Tante Lotte gave orders to immediately hitch Iwan to the lighter wagon. We were going to go back and get Mama, Herbert and Opa!

Early the next morning we started back to Pogress. It was so nice to not have to walk this time. Tante Lotte and Walter came with Harry and me and we had a nice time visiting on our way back. It was another beautiful spring day. We travelled hard and fast all day. Iwan was a strong horse and seemed to never tire. Tante Lotte said we should travel straight through without stopping until we got to Mama. We arrived late in the evening on the same path we had left from. Mama stood at the same spot as when we left. I wondered how often she stood there and looked towards where she'd seen us last. Mama was so happy she wept tears of joy and relief. I'm sure she was terribly worried about us going off alone like that. All I can remember about that night was all of us lying on the floor and Mama and Tante Lotte talking long into the night.

In the morning we got ready to go. There wasn't much to pack. We just got dressed and got on the wagon. But there were dear friends we had made in that short space of time and Mama wanted to say good-bye to them and to thank different folks for all they had done for us. Mama also went to say good-bye to the Burgermeister (mayor), too. He told Mama that things didn't look very good. He really didn't think we'd be able to get back to Luebeck, especially with a horse and wagon. He gave Mama some advice. He told her to go to Zarentin to the Embassy and talk with a man there about obtaining a travelling permit, which might help us make it back to Luebeck.

On our way back, we stopped in Zarentin and Mama went to the British military office. She told them our whole story and situation. Suddenly, the man's eyes got big and he became very excited. He asked Mama if she had sent two Canadian kids named Ruth and Harry to get help from an aunt in Luebeck. Mama was puzzled, but she said they were and wanted to know how he knew about them? "Well," he answered, "I'm the one who picked them up on the road that night and gave them a ride." Again, Mama shed tears of joy and thanksgiving. She was so overjoyed to meet this "good Samaritan," she could have kissed his feet but his kindness and help didn't end there. He helped us even more. He told Mama, "I'm going to give you a permit to travel with the horse and wagon. I will also put down that you are a Canadian citizen, which will enable you to get through the road blocks that have been set up."

We had been waiting for Mama in the wagon. When she came back and told us all about meeting the man who had helped us and that he had given us a travelling permit, we were all so happy and thankful. By this time it was getting late and considering the situation with the roadblocks, we didn't have much time. We left immediately without any delays. We knew we wouldn't be able to get all the way to Luebeck, by nightfall, anymore, no matter how fast we drove the poor horse.

Everything went smoothly until we arrived in Ratzeburg. There, we ran into our first roadblock. A lake divides the city of Ratzeburg and they had put the roadblock on the bridge. They stopped us and told us we could not go through. Mama showed them our permit. They examined it, returned it to her and still said we could not go through. They looked at us suspiciously. I think they did not believe we were really Canadians. They said we were allowed to cross the bridge but would have to leave the horse and wagon behind. Then they changed their minds and said they would check with the authorities and see whether we could cross over in the morning with the horse and wagon.

We were confronted with a dilemma. We didn't want Tante Lotte to lose her horse and wagon after coming this far. So we decided to stay with the horse and wagon and she and Walter would cross the bridge and spend the night on that side. That way, in case they didn't allow us to cross in the morning, they would be safe. So Tante Lotte and Walter crossed the bridge and slept in a school on the other side while we stayed with the wagon.

First thing in the morning, Mama met and talked with the guard. He said that because of the new ordinances he couldn't allow us to go across with the horse and wagon...only on foot. No one was allowed to bring horses or wagons across now. While we were waiting for Tante Lotte and Walter to cross back over and join us, Mama complained to some British soldiers about the stupidity of the blockade. They told her about a country back road that was about twelve kilometres out of the way. It, also, had a roadblock, but he thought, if we hurried, we might make it through before they received word of the new ordinances.

As soon as Tante Lotte and Walter arrived we all left immediately. Walter drove fast and soon the horse was soaked with sweat. As we approached the roadblock, we slowed to a trot because we were worried the authorities might think we were running away from something. They stopped us and started asking us questions. Mama answered them and showed them our permit. The rest of us didn't say a single word. We just sat there looking nonchalant, holding our collective breath and saying silent prayers. The guards handed the permit around to each other and then came over and searched the wagon. Then, to our great relief, they said we could go. It was difficult to hide our happiness and not look over-joyed until we were out of sight. At this point, we knew in our hearts that we had made it. *Really* made it this time!! We didn't stop. We knew Tante Mitze would be anxiously waiting for us. It was a joyous reunion but also a sad one. I'm sure poor Iwan was glad to be back at the farm, too. It was a strenuous workout for him.

We stayed at Tante Mitze's since we had nowhere else to go. (Do you remember, Karin, the size of Tante Mitze's place?) It wasn't very big—a medium sized bedroom, small living room, a very small kitchen and a tiny bathroom. Of course, Tante Mitze hadn't needed much room for just herself and Onkel Georg. They had no children. But now there were five of us, plus Tante Lotte, Walter and Oma Schoenberg, which made ten people, living in those three little rooms. But, it was a place to stay.

Tante Lotte had all her belongings unloaded there, too. There was so much stuff, you couldn't clean up or put anything away because there was no empty space to put anything. It was such a mess! Not only was the space situation a problem, but food was a bigger problem. We didn't have anything– no money at all, not even one pfennig, with which we could help buy food—all we had were the clothes on our backs. Even if we did have some money, there was still very little food available…and what small amount you did find in the stores could only be purchased with food stamps. Petro, the Italian prisoner who had come with Tante Lotte, had to go to a prison camp operated by the British, but he was to be released in a few weeks to go back to Italy to his family. He was very nice and we were all going to miss him. We had become such good friends, even while still on the farm in West Prussia.

ESSEN 507	A ⑤ 11 Febr.	B ③ 11 Febr.	B ② 11 Febr.	B ① 11 Febr.	HESSEN 407	A 5 11 Jan.	B 3 11 Jan.	B 2 11 Jan.	B 1 11 Jan.
L 11 ESSEN 508	H 11 Febr.	B ⓿ 11 Febr.	T 36 11 Febr.	T 35 11 Febr.	L 11 HESSEN 408	D * 11 Jan.	B 4 11 Jan.	T 2 11 Jan.	T 1 11 Jan.
Bundes-republik Deutschland LEA ESSEN	100 g W-Brot 11 Febr.	100 g W-Brot 11 Febr.	G 11 Febr.	500 g W-Brot 11 Febr. 6	500 g W-Brot 11 Febr. 5	Bundesrepublik Deutschland LEA HESSEN	100g W-Brot 11 Jan.	100 g W-Brot 11 Jan.	C * 11 Jan.	500 g W-Brot 11 Jan. 2	500 g W-Brot 11 Jan. 1
E 35 wachsene 16 Jahre Februar 1950	100 g W-Brot 11 Febr.	100 g W-Brot 11 Febr.	100 g W-Brot 11 Febr.	100 g W-Brot 11 Febr.	100 g W-Brot 11 Febr.	100 g W-Brot 11 Febr.	100 g W-Brot 11 Febr.	100 g W-Brot 11 Febr.	E 134 Erwachsene ab.16 Jahre Januar 1950	100 g W-Brot 11 Jan.	100 g W-Brot 11 Jan.	100 g W-Brot 11 Jan.	100 g W-Brot 11 Jan.	100 g W-Brot 11 Jan.	100 g W-Brot 11 Jan.	100 g W-Brot 11 Jan.	100 g W-Brot 11 Jan.
	FETT R 11 Febr.	BU ㉓ 11 Febr.	BU 22 11 Febr.	125 g Butter 11 Febr. 17		FETT R 11 Jan.	Bu ⑥ 11 Jan.	Bu ⑤ 11 Jan.	125 g Butter 11 Jan. 1
11	FETT 11 S Febr.	250g Fett 11 Febr. C	250g Fett 11 Febr. B	250g Fett 11 Febr. A		FETT S 11 Jan.	250g Fett ⑪ Jan. C	250g Fett ⑪ Jan. B	250g Fett ⑪ Jan. A
11	15 ⑪ Febr. ZUCKER	500 g Zucker 11 Febr. ⑬	500 g Zucker 11 Febr. ⑫		11	3 11 Jan. ZUCKER	500 g Zucker 11 Jan. 2	500 g Zucker 11 Jan. 1
Z 11 ESSEN 503	Z 11 HESSEN 305	Fleisch 27 11 Febr.	Fleisch 26 11 Febr.	Fleisch 25 11 Febr.	Z 11 HESSEN 403	Z 11 HESSEN 405	Fleisch 7 11 Jan.	Fleisch 6 11 Jan.	Fleisch 5 11 Jan.
Z 11 ESSEN	Z 11 HESSEN	Fleisch 11 23	125 g FLEISCH	125 g FLEISCH	Z 11 HESSEN	Z 11 HESSEN	Fleisch 4 11	125 g FLEISCH	125 g FLEISCH

Food stamps: *fleisch*-meat/sausage, *fett*-lard, *brot*-bread, *BU*- butter, and *zucker*-sugar (450 grams equals 1 pound).

Harry and I in front of the army barracks in Vorrade where we lived from May 1945 until May 1946.

Herbert in front of the barracks.

Mama and Papa in KL. Zecher.

Norbert and I.

The Blunk's home in Soehren, where I did
my apprenticeship in home economics.

Ellen at five months old in Kl. Zecher.

My family in Kl. Zecher in 1947.

Harry and I in Luebeck in 1947.

My girlfriends, Marga and Edith,
and I with Rosebrock's horses.

In Kl. Zecher, milking the cows in the pasture, 1948.

My favorite cow, Irene, in 1948.

Me at sixteen years old.

Herbert, Ellen and Greif in
Kl. Zecher in 1948.

Mama and Papa gave Harry and I an
accordion before we left for Canada.

Paper was used instead of coins at
this time. This is a sample of the
front and back of a nickle.

This is a sample of
the front and back
of the currency.

CHAPTER 13
SURVIVING IN LUEBECK

A few days after we arrived there and had settled in, Mama scouted around Luebeck looking for a solution to our living arrangements and lack of food and money. We were all in limbo. She went to a Displaced Persons' Bureau again and they gave her some food stamps and some money, but now, the stores had no food left. The few groceries that arrived in the shops in the morning were all snatched up in the first two hours. The people who arrived there first got food and the rest went away empty handed. People came before dawn to wait in line. As daylight came one could see people sitting on little folding chairs or standing and waiting for the store to open. They would stand for many hours hoping to get some food.

We knew we couldn't stay at Tante Mitze's and Onkel Georg's much longer. A committee in charge of living quarters told Mama that there was an army camp not far from Luebeck that was vacant and that there were many barracks available for those who got there first. Mama left immediately. When she got there, people were already living in most of them. A Red Cross supervisor, who was responsible for the refugees, told her there were none available at that site, but he had one empty barrack at the bottom of the hill. Even though it had no windows, Mama took it so we would have a place to stay. She thought we could leave the door open for light to come in. We moved in the next day. All we had to do was walk in because we had nothing. Tante Lotte gave us a featherbed and a blanket. We found some gunny sacks, filled them with straw and used them for our beds. Opa and Mama gathered some bricks, laid them together to make a stove with an opening at the top to set a pan or pot on. Opa cut a hole in the wall with a pipe so the smoke could escape, but there was always some smoke that remained inside. We had no household utensils. The Red Cross supervisor told us about another army camp we could go to and they would give us many of the utensils we needed. Mama talked to Tante Lotte and she let us use Iwan and the wagon. Mama and Opa went to the army camp and brought back all the things we needed: bed frames made of raw boards, aluminum pots and pans that were dented and sooty from fires but, at least, there were no holes in them, some dishes and aluminum knives, forks and spoons that bent easily…but, we were so happy to have these things.

Mama even brought home a box full of nylon parachute material. It was striped light and dark green. Later, she made clothing out of it for us. We had underwear, petticoats and dresses all made out of the same material. Harry, Grandpa and Herbert had pants and coats made from German army uniforms that had to be dyed before wearing.

During this process, Mama made friends with some more soldiers. There were Canadian and British soldiers in this sector. We met them often when we walked into town. A couple of Canadian soldiers used to come over, visit us and bring oranges. They would ask Mama if there was anything we needed. When she told them we had no soap or matches, they brought them. How wonderful it was to be able to make a fire! We gathered sticks in the woods and used old boards or anything else we could find that would fit in the stove and burn. If they didn't fit, we would prop them up against something and stomp on them until they broke. We had to take turns breaking them because our feet would get so sore… especially being barefoot or wearing shoes with wooden soles.

We soon discovered that other people had no matches or any way of starting a fire either, because soon after we had a fire and the smoke was pouring out of the chimney, we heard a knock at the door. A lady a few barracks down from ours asked if she could have some hot coal to start a fire. It ended up that this was how the whole neighbourhood started their fires each morning. They would wait until they could see the smoke coming from our chimney and then they would come with a little shovel or a piece of tin to get some hot embers.

Now our biggest problem was trying to acquire food and wood. No one had a clock, so we just lived from daylight to daylight. It was difficult to keep track of the date and we often didn't know what day it was. We went to town early each day to stand in line to get food. We got very little. On the way to town and back we passed fields of vegetables. We decided to get some of them to eat. In the daytime we saw fields that had vegetables and we would choose one that we thought would be easy to sneak into, then we would go back at night. Mama, Harry or I would go and dig up some vegetables. Sometimes it was carrots, sometimes beets or cabbage. We would eat that one item until it was gone and then go back and try to get something else. We always tried to get enough so we wouldn't have to go back for a couple of nights. Mama would cook whatever we got in water and we would eat them morning, noon and night. Sometimes in the mornings we would cut off the heads of ripening wheat in the fields. We would rub the seeds out and grind them in the coffee grinder (we had received one from Tante Lotte) to cook into a kind of porridge.

Every time we had something to eat that tasted better than usual, Mama wouldn't eat with us. When we asked her why she wasn't eating, she would tell us she had eaten while she was cooking. It took us a long time to discover that at those times she wasn't eating at all so there would be enough for the rest of us.

There *never* seemed to be a shortage of brusselsprouts! I'll tell you why. You see, because we weren't the only ones who were going out at night digging up vegetables the farmers began guarding their fields. The punishment for stealing food was going to jail for a long time. The *only* reason we stole was because we were so very hungry…anyway, back to the brusselsprouts. We would sneak up to the fields on our hands and knees and when we saw someone in the distance we had to be very careful because we were never sure if it was someone else getting food or a guard. So, because of that fear, we ended up going to a field right near our barracks that happened to grow brusselsprouts. It was much easier to get in and out of. So, more times than not, we came home with brusselsprouts. Can you imagine eating brusselsprouts three times a day? Day after day?

Oh, ick! Now you know why I still hate even the thought of brusselsprouts to this day!

After we had lived in the barracks for about four weeks, a family moved out of the one beside us. They either went to live with relatives or were hired by a farmer, I can't remember exactly. Anyway, Mama went to see the Red Cross supervisor and he said we could have that barrack. We quickly moved into it. It had two rooms and two windows, so now we had daylight. There was, also, a good-sized shed outside where we could store things. We were much happier living there. At night we continued our foraging trips to the adjacent fields. We, also, discovered a pasture that had milk cows. They were quite tame, so we would take a little pail or pot and milk them. Some of them wouldn't stand still and when they saw us coming, they would run. But, many of them weren't afraid and when it was dark and they were lying down, we would slowly sneak in among the herd and quietly talk to them. Eventually we would get a cow to stand up so we could milk her. While one of us was milking, the other stood watch. Sometimes the farmers would go around checking, so if we saw someone coming, we took off running as fast as we could! Sometimes, we would only be running away from others who were out for the same purpose. But, we were so fearful of being caught by the police or farmers; we were extra cautious and ran away to be on the safe side.

Some farmers began complaining about the problem to the British so they sent troops out at night to check the fields. One night Mama and I came out of the pasture where we had taken some milk. We were heading for the road when we heard the sound of approaching trucks. Mama and I quickly hid in a hedge that ran parallel with the road. We crawled into the hedge as far as we could and sat in the thickest part with the precious pot of milk held between our knees. We saw the headlights of the trucks come around the bend in the road. There were about five or six trucks with many soldiers in each of them. Since the roads in Germany are very narrow, they passed within one and a half to two metres[17] from us. We crouched there, hearts pounding, with tears streaming down our cheeks, scarcely daring to breathe and praying to God for help. The trucks and all the soldiers jumped off and began walking around, laughing and relieving themselves. We were so sure that it was over...that we were caught but, they didn't see us. After a short while, they jumped back on the trucks and left. Mama and I sat there for a long, long time, thanking the Lord for protecting us, before we moved to go home. After that, we didn't go there again for a long time. Not only did people get punished for stealing vegetables and milk...they were also punished for disobeying the curfew...a 6:00 p.m. curfew was in effect, so no civilians were allowed to be out of their homes after that time. So, we would have been in double the trouble if we'd been caught.

Not too long after that horrifying experience, I became very ill with yellow jaundice.[18] It was another terrible time for all of us. I had a difficult time recovering and was sick for a long time...probably three weeks or so. Because I was so ill I have difficulties remembering this period of time. I do know that we had a friend who was a medic in the military and I believe he came and tried to help us. He told us that there wasn't anything that could be done because of the scarcity of doctors and medicine. Mama brought lots and lots of whole milk for me to drink believing that this would help me gain weight and strength and help me heal. I have learned since that it is a miracle that I recovered so well...and we thanked our Lord once again for his healing touch.

Mama went to town many mornings extremely early to stand in line at the butcher shop. She used all her meat stamps to buy horsemeat. Because we were willing to eat horsemeat, we were able to get triple the amount of meat with our stamps. Every time she went to town, she visited Tante Mitze's to see if, maybe, Tante Lotte had heard from Onkel Wilhelm or, maybe, Papa had shown up or someone had left word notifying us he was alive and safe. We couldn't accept the fact that he could be dead. She, also, went to the Red Cross and sent a telegram to our relatives in Canada and in Detroit telling them that we had survived and where we were staying, so that in case Papa should contact them looking for us, they could pass this information on to him. No mail was leaving Germany and the only way we could send a letter or receive one was through the Red Cross. Our relatives in North America responded and said they had not heard from Papa. They said they were going to help us by sending us parcels with some food and clothing...what a blessing! These were the only care packages we received.

We didn't know where any of our other 'refugee' relatives were so we couldn't contact them. Many families were broken apart and scattered and didn't know the fate of their relatives. Most families weren't as fortunate as we were. Many of them were searching for their children or parents or husbands or wives. The Red Cross published a displaced persons newspaper to help people locate one another. A person gave their name, the name of their family, their last address in the East and their present address. This information was listed alphabetically in newspapers that were left in piles in convenient places where people could find them. It made it much easier to locate friends, relatives or neighbors. Every week the list got longer and longer until it had become a thick "book-like" document. Your name appeared every week until you found the people you were looking for then your name was withdrawn from the list.

About this time Herbert became very ill. Large ulcerated boils broke out on his face and neck. We were so worried! Mama told the British soldier, the one that brought us oranges, about Herbert. He made arrangements for Mama to take Herbert to the doctor on the army base in Blankensee. When Mama took Herbert to the base she had problems with the guard at the gate. He refused to let her enter. After some discussion and information, Mama was finally allowed through. The doctor said Herbert must come for several follow up visits so he could give him penicillin shots…after the treatments he improved rapidly. When Mama went to the doctor's appointments, she often visited with the guard. When he learned that she had lived in Winnipeg, he told her he was from St. Boniface in Winnipeg. A happy result…Mama made a new acquaintance and Herbert recovered completely.

We take so many little things in life for granted. One day Mama brought home a clock that Tante Lotte had given her and we were absolutely delighted that now we would know what time it was. We set the clock in the window so all our neighbors could share this little luxury. It seemed as if, little by little, things were getting better…but, oh so slowly. I was slowly recovering from the jaundice. We were beginning to discover resourceful ways of getting food. Through friendships Mama had made, she was able to trade some of the soap we got from the British for extra bread stamps. A 'fish lady' lived halfway between our home and Luebeck.

She peddled fish around the countryside and she would, occasionally, give Mama some pieces of cod.

One day in July, a woman brought a note to Tante Mitze's place. These words were scribbled on the note: *Gneisenauer. Str. 49. Bring me some bread. Wilhelm.* After Tante Lotte read the note she said, "That is my husband! Where did you get that note?" The woman answered, "There was a large troop of German soldiers walking through the city and one of them gave it to me." (We found out later they were all war prisoners who were being moved on foot, fifty-six kilometres, from Hamburg to Bad Segeberg.) Tante Lotte asked what he looked like. She said he was wounded with bandages on his head and knee and limping with a cane. Tante Lotte grabbed some bread and ran to find him. She came back home distraught. She said she could not find them or see them anywhere. However, four days later Onkel Wilhelm walked in the door!! He had been a prisoner of war under the British, who had rounded up all the German soldiers and marched them to the releasing camp in Bad Segeberg. He said that he had been fighting in East Prussia and was wounded in the middle of June. They had received no word that the war had ended on May 5th. The Russians surrounded them and they fiercely fought against them not knowing the war had long ended. He was able to get on a boat from there to Sweden where he finally heard the news: THE WAR IS OVER!

What a bittersweet reunion it was!! After Onkel Wilhelm regained his strength, he went looking for a job. He knew that they couldn't stay with Tante Mitze much longer. He found work on a farm not far from Luebeck that provided living quarters for his whole family. They even let him bring his team of horses along, except for Iwan. Nobody wanted him. So, Mama said we'd take care of him if we could have the little "Panja"[19] wagon, too. We decided to keep him until Onkel Wilhelm wanted to sell him. We used that shed behind our barracks as a barn for Iwan. After that, things got better for us.

Mama went back to the British embassy and they gave us a permit for food supplies for the horse. We, also, herded him along the roadsides where there was tall grass growing. After we had Iwan for awhile, the fish lady noticed that we had a horse and she asked if we would like to have a job hauling fish. I told Mama…that's the job for me!! I loved horses and

I loved to drive! So, Mama gave me permission to do it. Two days a week I went with the fish lady, Frau Schuneman, to the harbour in Luebeck to meet the freighter where we picked up the fish. Then we would drive to little towns and villages on her route and peddle the fish for meat stamps. We would drive into each town very slowly and she would ring a bell and yell at the top of her lungs, "Fresh fish! Fresh fish!" At the end of the day, if there were some fish left over, she would give me some to take home. And, of course, the fish that was left at the end of the day was cod. I got almost as sick of cod as I did of brusselsprouts! Mama, with her sharp sense of business, took some of the fish and traded it for bread. In this way, we often had bread when other people didn't and the baker had fish, which he wanted.

When little Herbert went outside to play Mama would often give him a sandwich to take with him. This wasn't a sandwich like you are accustomed to; this was a slice of bread with sugar sprinkled on it. The other kids, not having any bread, would wait for him to come out and then they would take the bread away from him and eat it. Herbert would come in crying, telling Mama what happened. But Mama never said anything. She would just make him another slice of bread. Opa, however, was furious! He would bawl Mama out for letting him go outside with it. He'd say, "It's almost our last piece of bread. What are we going to eat tomorrow?" But, Mama would quietly say, "Let them eat what we have today and God will take care of tomorrow"…and God always did. Sometimes some days weren't as good as others, but there was always something to eat. Mama's faith was so strong and she'd say, "We live just for today…one day at a time." And it worked.

We had a lot of trouble finding wood. Having the horse helped, because we could drive to the forest to gather branches. We were only allowed to pick dry branches that were lying on the ground. Live trees wouldn't burn because of their moisture while the dried branches burned easily. But, remember, everyone was gathering branches so, soon, we couldn't even find a branch that was as thick as our finger. The woods were picked as clean as a garden. Then, someone figured out how to get the dead branches down that were still attached to the trees. We got a long stick and put a hook on the end. With this, we reached high into the trees hooking the dry branches and pulling them down. If they were dead, they would break off. You weren't allowed to saw any limbs off the trees unless you had a permit. Everyone was allowed one tree a season to cut for wood. That wasn't very much when you took into consideration the fact that it was used for heating and cooking. While gathering branches we were always on the lookout for dead trees. When we found one, we'd mark the route there, so we could go back another, more convenient day and saw the whole thing down. We'd, then, work very quickly (as this was illegal) to cut it into pieces small enough to fit in the wagon snugly. We'd cover it up with small branches and bring it home. Mama used to talk to us, explaining to us that stealing the way we did to survive, would not be a sin, especially if we asked God's forgiveness. She said we must never steal more than we needed for our survival. God must have forgiven us, too, because we never got caught although it was very close sometimes! Mama used to talk about God a lot.

The summer of 1945 passed by and autumn arrived. Life began to take on a more normal routine. I had my pigtails cut off. I had wanted them cut, but after they were gone, I cried. Mama sent me to a sewing school to become an apprentice. She wanted me to be a dressmaker. I went for one week and, then, begged Mama not to make me go anymore because I hated sewing so very much. We looked around for a job doing housework. She, also, tried to get Harry back into school, but the school wasn't in session yet.

One day we received a letter from a man who had found Mama's name in the Displaced Persons paper. This is what he wrote:

> I saw your name and address and read that you are looking for Johann Garn. I was his buddy and fought and walked beside him and I want to give you the sad news that he was killed in the forest by Lessen, West Prussia, where we were fighting. He did not suffer. A grenade tore away his chest and identification and you will probably get a notice some day of him listed as "missing in action." I don't want you to get your hopes up. We were unable to bury any of the dead because we had to retreat quickly and the dead all fell into Russian hands. Don't try to write to me because I just found my

wife and children's names in this paper, too. I see they are in East Berlin. So, tonight, I will go "black" (sneaking) across the border to be with them. Maybe someday we will figure something out so that all of us can come back to the Western Zone.

That made it final. Mama was brokenhearted and so were we. We cried and cried, realizing that Papa would never ever be coming back to us. Mama took the letter to the courthouse in Luebeck to record his death and to receive a death certificate. It was still too difficult for me to accept and I continued to look for him everywhere I went. Whenever I saw a lone man, I thought to myself, "Maybe, just maybe, it is Papa"…but it never was.

Onkel Wilhelm came over one day and said he had a buyer for Iwan and had decided to sell him. I was, again, very, very sad. I was so attached to that horse by now and it was so hard to give him up. Onkel Wilhelm said that he had, also, sold one of the team horses. He wanted to know if we'd like to have the horse that was left. I was glad but a little worried, too. The horse's name was Norbert. He was young, more spirited and a lot bigger than Iwan so this meant he ate a lot more food, too.

Shortly after getting Norbert, I had a terrifying experience. On the third day after we had Norbert, I took him out to eat grass along the roadside late in the afternoon but before the 6:00 p.m. curfew. I took him around a bend in the road, which blocked the view of home, but we went there because there was a lot of nice grass for him. I enjoyed standing watch over Norbert as he ate, and as I watched, I hummed and sang to myself and to the horse. Opa always said that horses liked to hear singing.

As I stood there singing, I saw a man walking down the slope. He stared at me while he was walking towards me. I got a strange feeling as he came closer, and I moved to the other side of the horse. This way, he would pass me with the horse between us. He walked past me around the bend but kept turning around and looking at me. Soon he was gone and I sighed with relief. I was shaking like a leaf, I was so scared.

I decided it was time to go home…besides it was close to suppertime. As I started around the bend, the same man came back again. I was terrified. I stopped and didn't know what to do. I thought maybe I should run.

But, Norbert was so big and slow I figured that it wouldn't be such a good idea. Besides, there wasn't any place to run to. A hedge of thorny bushes was growing along each side of the road and there was only one opening which led to a lane leading into a field. I decided I would just have to pass him. My heart was pounding with terror and I was shaking all over! I was so frightened! I tried switching sides again in order to pass him, but every time I switched, he did, too. Now I knew I was in real danger and I was all alone. I had never felt so alone in all my life as I did then. Just as he got really close, I quickly changed sides again, hoping I could slip past him with the horse between us. But, just as I thought I had made it and sighed with relief, he stepped behind the horse and came up behind me. He grabbed me by my throat. With one hand around my throat so tight his fingers dug into my skin choking me and his other arm and hand around my body, he dragged me down to the lane leading into the field. The rope from Norbert's halter was wrapped around my hands and he let loose of my throat for a quick moment in an effort to free them, but kept telling me, "If you scream, I'll kill you!" I tried to pull his hand loose, because I couldn't breathe. All of a sudden, I thought I heard someone calling in the distance, "Ruth, come home for supper!"

Hearing that snapped me out of my shock and I found the strength to scream. I screamed and screamed with all the strength I had and as loud as I could over and over and over. Suddenly the man dropped me and ran behind the hedges. I lay there on the ground screaming and crying hysterically when Harry and Heine, a friend and neighbor boy, came running. Bending over me, they wondered what had happened. They had heard me screaming and thought Norbert had hurt me somehow, so they ran as fast as they could. The man must have run away while they were checking on my condition. After I told them what had happened, they went to look for him and he was nowhere to be found. Harry and Heine helped me up and helped me to get home.

Mama was so shocked when she heard what had happened to me and even more shocked when she saw how I looked. My throat was severely swollen and I had marks all over my neck which later, turned black and blue. Oh, how I thanked the Lord for sending Harry and Heine to my rescue. I never went out alone again after that. I didn't even walk to town in the daytime alone. We all walked in groups after that. It was a terrible and frightening experience. Because of the many war prisoners that had been freed, this was becoming a common danger.

We didn't have Norbert very long because Onkel Wilhelm found someone who wanted to buy him, too. We thought it was for the best because winter was coming and Mama was trying to find a place for me to go to work.

Around that time, a man occasionally came to visit us in the evenings. Mama told us he was a friend who she had met while walking to town. He had approached her and asked if she had cigarette stamps to give or sell. She told him, "You can have the cigarette coupons in exchange for food." He said he would give her milk since he worked on a dairy farm. They began talking more and Mama found out that he had been in the army on the Russian front. Originally he was from Konigsberg, East Prussia. He had a wife and five children (four boys and one girl). The girl was the youngest at only two years old. Through some friends, he had found out that while his family was fleeing, they got as far as Danzig in West Prussia when the Russians surrounded them. The only way out was across the Baltic Sea by ship. This ship was named the *Gustloff* (We found out later, this ship was torpedoed by the Russians and sank killing over 10,000 people...mostly civilians (women and children) and wounded German soldiers. This is still, today, the largest and most horrible sea disaster of all time). This man who befriended Mama was Emil Sprung.

Emil came often and brought us food to eat. He was a Schweitzer, which is a person who takes care of dairy cattle. He had access to a variety of foods and brought us milk, eggs and other stuff. We knew the farmer didn't give them and that they were stolen. Emil started looking out for our welfare. He even managed to drag a little calf out of the barn into the woods where he butchered it. He brought us the meat and we tried to cut it up in the dark of the night. I'll never forget when we ate that meat. We ate and ate as much as we could. Mama preserved some in salt but I can't remember what she did with the rest of it so it wouldn't spoil.

CHAPTER 14
SOEHREN, KR. SEGEBERG

Not too long after that, we saw an ad in the paper that said a farmer from Soehren Kr. Segeberg was looking for a female apprentice in the field of home economics. Mama felt that would be a good place for me. I wouldn't earn much money, but I could get a diploma after four years. An apprentice is kept more like a member of the family. Mama didn't care what the pay was, as long as I had a good place to stay and had food to eat.

We applied for the position, sending them the information they needed. After a few days we received a reply. They wanted us to come for an interview. Since it was quite a distance we took the train. Someone picked us up at the train station with a horse and buggy. The buggy had rubber tires which I thought was quite special. We arrived at the Blunk's farm in Soehren quite late in the evening, long after suppertime, but we were given a meal anyway. I remember eating little potatoes fried nice and brown in butter. I don't remember what else we had to eat, but those little potatoes were *so good*! I can almost taste them today and I don't think potatoes will ever taste as good again!! I remember eating like I had never eaten before. I must have just wolfed them down barely chewing!

We had to spend the night since there was only one train a day. Frau Blunk asked all kinds of questions and we talked a lot. The next morning over breakfast she told us that she had decided to take me over twenty-five other applicants. She said she liked the way I answered her questions and that I looked like I would be a good worker. She said, "I can always tell a good worker by the way she eats. A fast eater is usually a fast worker." However, she really didn't know if I ate fast because I was hungry or if I ate fast because I was a fast worker.

She showed us around the farm right after breakfast because shortly after noon, we had to catch our train to go home. The tour of their farm reminded us, once again, of the farm we had left behind and all we had lost. The pain was indescribable...but we had to learn to accept it. A week later I returned to the Blunk's to stay.

It was so painful to leave my family. Herbert was only two years old and I loved him so much. I wouldn't be able to play with him everyday like I was used to doing. It was so hard to leave Harry, too. We had gone through so much together. Sure we had our share of disagreements, but no more than any other brother and sister. We hardly went anywhere without going together. Oh, and Mama...how could I ever leave her? She had gone through so much hardship and worry and all the responsibility of her family's lives was on her shoulders. She was so thin and her face looked so drawn. The only time we ever saw her smile was when she looked at us. The love she had for us shone through her sad, tired eyes. I loved her so much but I knew I had to go and that it was the best thing for me. I was still only thirteen years old and it was so difficult to cope with all that had happened in less than a year.

When I arrived at the train depot someone from the Blunk's farm was there to pick me up. At the farm, I shared a room with a girl named Hella. She was two years older than I was and very nice. She was working on her last two years of apprenticeship and had grown up in the West. Her folks had a large farm not too far from there and she couldn't comprehend what it meant to lose everything you owned, to flee with nothing but the clothing on your back, experience starvation and freezing weather and not have enough to wear to stay warm. In spite of that we got along well together.

To me, being at the Blunk's farm was like being in paradise. They had such a big house filled with marvelous furniture. Everything was quite fancy. But their beautiful house was, also, a full house. The Blunk's had three refugee families living in their house as well as their own family *and* their hired help. West Germany had required its citizens to give up all extra space in their homes for refugees. The Blunk family had, for their own use, the kitchen and three bedrooms (one for the males, one for the females and one for Frau and Herr Blunk). We had such a soft bed to sleep in and a feather quilt to cover up with. It almost seemed too good to be true. I couldn't believe it was happening to me. There was always good food to eat and meals were on a regular basis. Everything was *so* nice there. I felt guilty being in this place while my family was struggling to keep warm and have enough to eat.

Because it was a large farm, it required two male apprentices along with other hired help to get all the work done. There was a full table at mealtimes…usually nine to eleven people. We girls had to learn how to do everything. Wintertime was coming and we cleaned and mended and knitted and worked on special projects. We, also, had to learn how to clean and dry the wool after the sheep had been sheared. We learned how to spin the wool and after that we knitted. However, we weren't allowed to keep most of the wool, meat, chickens or pork. It was all controlled by the government and we were only allowed to keep a designated amount (because the government had issued food stamps to everyone, they regulated all of the food supply…animal and vegetable…so that no one would have an advantage over anyone else). However, when you owned your own farm there was always a way to get around these regulations.

We were all treated like members of the family and they told us everything that went on, but we were expected to be loyal and never say anything to anyone and to help protect them if necessary. And we did… as we too considered ourselves part of the family. We used to take some cream off the milk before it was shipped and then let it sour. We'd take turns in the cellar making butter. We'd make it in an old cream can and would wrap a rug around it so it wouldn't make any noise. One of us would always keep watch. You never knew when a government inspector might come around…there were regulations that determined the amount of butter, cream or milk we could keep for ourselves.

When it was time to butcher, all the animals were counted and we were allowed to butcher and keep our quota as per our food stamps. But Herr and Frau Blunk managed to raise a pig or calf secretly to butcher for their own use. We made most of the meat into sausage because that was the best way to hide it plus it kept better that way. We did all our work at night. We blacked out the windows in the room where we worked. The Blunk's were such nice people. They were strict but they showed a lot of love, too.

Normally, we had to be asleep every night by nine o'clock in the summer and ten o'clock in winter…not only in bed, but also *asleep*. In the winter, we had to be up by 6:00 a.m. and in the summer at 5:00 a.m. I was beginning to feel at home there, but many nights I cried myself to sleep because I missed my family so much!

This is another year without Christmas…still too much turmoil…

In early 1946, Frau Blunk said that I could go home for a weekend. Oh, how happy I was!! I had been at the Blunks' for five months now. She hired a dressmaker to sew some new clothes for me. She even had a couple of her own dresses altered to fit me. When I was ready to go home, I felt like Cinderella. The ride home was the longest I had ever taken. I thought I was never going to get home! When my family and I finally saw each other, we wept with happiness at being together once again.

Things hadn't changed much at home. The food shortage was the same. Mama was very happy over some things Frau Blunk had sent along for them. The two days at home flew by too fast and it seemed like only minutes before it was time to go back again. The pain was there all over again, especially at night. It was so difficult to be so far away from my dear family.

One day in April, Frau Blunk called me to her room and asked me to sit on her lap as she had something special to tell me. She said she had received a letter from my Mama. I was so positive that something terrible had happened at home that I felt like screaming and running away or rolling on the floor to shut out the bad news. The fear and pain welled up in my heart so fiercely, I could hardly stand it…I held my breath. Sensing my distress, Frau Blunk said, "Ruth! It's good news!" I was so relieved! I listened carefully to what she had to tell me. She said that Mama was planning to get married. Even though she had told me the news so tenderly, I was still taken aback and I just sat there, completely thunderstruck. I finally asked, "To whom?" She told me Mama was marrying a man she had met some months ago who was lonely and wanted to help Mama care for her family. He had lost his entire family in the war in the eastern zone. And then it hit me. "Is it Emil Sprung?" I asked. "Yes." said Frau Blunk.

I just couldn't explain my feelings at that point to anyone. All I could think of was my Papa, and that no matter what the papers said, I still believed he was alive. But, then I swallowed all my mixed up feelings of doubt and betrayal and began to sort things through in my mind more rationally. Why shouldn't Mama remarry? Wouldn't it be easier for her and wouldn't it mean that there would be food on the table for everyone? After thinking about it for awhile, I was finally able to accept it as the best thing for everyone.

CHAPTER 15
KLEIN ZECHER

On May 18, 1946, I got on a train again and headed for home, only this time to attend Mama's wedding. Frau Blunk had made a dress for me out of a chiffon bedspread...it was pale green with dark green flowers. I carried a large bouquet of lily of the valley flowers in one hand and my gift for Mama in the other. The simple wedding was held in Luebeck with only members of our family there: Onkel Wilhelm, Tante Lotte, Walter, Tante Mitze, Onkel Georg and Opa. When the ceremony was over, Tante Mitze hosted a small reception. She had prepared a nice dinner...as nice as it could be with the food shortages and what little she had to work with. A couple of months earlier my new stepfather had accepted a job as a Schweitzer with a large dairy farm in Klein Zecher, about thirty kilometres southeast of Luebeck.

In the afternoon, we all took the train to Klein Zecher which was to be my family's new home. There were no passenger trains at that time yet, so we all went together in a cattle car. The kids thought it was a lot of fun. With the doors wide open, we sat down and let our feet dangle over the edge. We thought it was a great trip. I'm not sure what the adults thought though!!

It was a half-hour walk from the train depot to Klein Zecher. The dairy farm had a furnished house where the farm workers and their families lived. When we arrived we found a surprise party (prepared by the families that lived there and some of Emil's co-workers) waiting for us in the large attic (one room) upstairs where Mama and our new Papa were to live. The farmer and owner, Herr Rosebrock, had furnished some food. Someone started playing an accordion and people began to dance in the attic. Everyone was happy.

After a couple of days, I had to return to Blunk's. This time the parting was easier, knowing that Mama was happy and knowing that even though they were crowded together into one room, there would be enough food for them all. Opa and Harry set up a cot in the attic and they slept there, too. Mama had to help with milking the cows plus all the other farm chores. Opa and Harry took care of Herbert until Mama came in from the barn. At this time Harry was living at home. He had taken a job as an assistant to a blacksmith in a neighboring village. He worked there until gymnasium started in Ratzeburg in late fall.

After Mama's marriage, Frau Blunk let me go home more often. Every two or three months I went home for three or four days. I became accustomed to the new place my family called home and made friends with the other kids in the village. By this time, Harry and I were sixteen and fifteen years old and longed to be together with other young people our age.

While I lived and worked at the Blunk's, Frau Blunk sent the apprentices to a dancing class in the next village and we learned all the steps to many different dances. We used to practise in the kitchen during the long winter evenings. Frau Blunk would turn on her record player, have us line up in the kitchen and help us practise the dance steps. Those were such fun times! Whenever there was a dance in the community, Herr Blunk lent us their horse and buggy so we could drive to the town where the dance was being held. There were the four of us...the two male apprentices and two females...and sometimes Marga came along if she was home. Marga was the Blunks' daughter who was away at school most of the time. We all stayed together, at the dance, like brothers and sisters. We had to leave together and come home together because those were the rules of the house. These dances were held once a month and, because we had so much fun, we wished they were more frequent. Sometimes a movie would come in between the dances and, even though the movies kept us out later, we were allowed to go. We usually walked to and from the dances and movies, when they were in nearby villages, but it was fun and we didn't mind it.

When I went home to visit my parents, the rules were similar. If there was a dance during an evening I was home, all the village kids would go together in a group...only, there, we went on a trailer pulled by a tractor that belonged to one of the big farmers. If there was no dance being held in town, then we gathered together in one of the farmer's kitchens and while someone played the accordion we danced right there! They had such huge old-fashioned kitchens. Other evenings we stayed at home.

We often had company...friends of my parents' who were all in the same difficult situation as we were. Sometimes we would sing...often in harmony. We would sing many songs and our new Papa taught us some new ones, too. But, sometimes, when we were singing, tears would start running down his face, and he couldn't sing anymore. He was crying for his wife and five children who all perished in the war. Those were very sad and depressing evenings and at those times, I was glad to go back to the Blunk's. But, I felt so sorry for him! I thanked God that He had spared our family that much grief. We lost our Papa, but we still had each other. No one was left of Emil's family.

On January 13, 1947, Mama had a baby girl, born at home, and they named her Ellen. Because I was her godmother, Frau Blunk let me go home for Ellen's Baptism and I was allowed to stay a few extra days. It was hard to stay at home in such crowded quarters, especially now with a little baby, too. So, I slept at the home of a friend of Mama's. When Ellen was a few months old, Mama and Papa were given different living quarters in the same house. Now they were downstairs and had four rooms.

It was hard for Mama to get things for the baby. She made diapers out of a flannel sheet and was able to get a couple of shirts through a friend of Harry's who worked in a store. A nurse who worked for Lutheran Social Services gave Mama some bottles and nipples as a special thank you for a special favour Mama and Papa had done for her. Following is the story of the special "favour."

The nurse had come to Mama's house about a month before Ellen was born and needed to sneak across the border back to the East Side. (Whenever someone would sneak across the border, it was called going 'black.') She was looking for a child that belonged to one of her friends. This friend, the child's mother, had been killed and the child was supposed to be in the Eastern Zone of Germany. Since we lived a stone's throw from the border, Mama and Papa helped a lot of people sneak across. They'd take a wagon to a pasture near the border to milk the cows and would hide the person in the wagon. Russian guards would walk from one end of the field to the other. While milking and watching the guards, they would tell the person when it was safe to run across. This is how they helped the nurse across, as well. They told her that when it was time for her to come back she must do it the same way. She sneaked back across one week later. She *did* find the child, a six-year-old boy, in an orphanage. Once they got back to our house, Mama and Papa gave them milk to drink and breakfast to eat. They, also, helped them get to the train station so they could continue on their journey. The nurse returned the child to his Papa and three weeks later Mama received a package from the nurse with the baby supplies.

A lot of people tried to sneak across the border…especially, from the East to the West. They had no one to help them and tried to do it on their own. If they were seen by the Russian guards, they were warned only once by, "Halt!" If the person took one more step they were shot on the spot. I know Herr Rosebrock helped a lot of wounded people off the field to safety. Of course, it had to be done unnoticed or he could get shot, too. Many people lost their lives on those fields.

In 1947 we received some letters from our relatives in Winnipeg and Detroit. They wanted to know if Harry and I would like to come to the United States or Canada, and if so, they would start the procedures required to do the paperwork for us. They also sent us parcels of food and used clothing. We were so grateful to receive those packages! It wasn't long before our relatives in Canada began the preparations to secure papers for Harry and me to immigrate to Canada. Harry and I were already Canadian citizens so it made the paperwork simpler. Life was still very difficult in Germany and Mama felt we would have a better life in Canada.

Mama thought I should quit working at Blunk's and come home now that they had more space. They, also, needed extra help, as it was a struggle handling all the chores with the new baby plus milking and tending to forty-five cows. Mama never did regain her strength and food was still in very short supply. Mama knew how to stretch everything so we never went to bed hungry. Even when an egg cost $0.35 a piece! Mama raised about six hens and she would sell some of the eggs in order to buy other kinds of foods...or she would trade them on the black market for other things we needed.

The black market was in Luebeck and there you could get anything without coupons. You had to be able to pay or have something to trade. Most black market handlers were from neighboring countries. You had to be very careful not to get caught. The police were always on the watch for black market traders.

I ended my contract with the Blunk's and came home. It was difficult to leave them. After two years of living and working there, it had become like home to me. They all had been so nice to me, especially Herr and Frau Blunk. All three of us wept when I left. Even though I felt sad to leave them I, also, had a great yearning in my heart to be home with Mama. By going home now, I felt I would have some time to spend with them before leaving for Canada.

Harry wasn't living at home at this time. He was living in Luebeck by Tante Mitze's and was an apprentice in a pharmacy. So, because he was away, Mama was especially happy to have me home. I worked most of the time in the barn, helping milk cows and doing all the other work that needed to be done. With my help in the barn, Mama was able to go home earlier to be with Herbert and Ellen and get her work finished there. Opa wasn't too well, either. He had started to fail again, and needed someone to look after him.

Winters were much more difficult than summers. Typically we received little snow, but the temperature often fell to freezing at night. There was always so much more to do in the winter because of the barn work. The livestock was kept inside during the winter months and this required hauling hay and mangels,[20] for them to eat, into the barn and removing manure out of the barn every day...heavy work!

It was now Christmas of 1947. Precious Christmas! When I think of Christmas I remember the tree. It was usually about one metre tall or a little more and we would put it on a table. It was decorated on Christmas

Eve day and we would help if we were home. It was decorated with home-made things like cookies, candies and a few Christmas balls. We always put white candles into little metal clips and put them on the tree. We lighted them on Christmas Eve and the evening of Christmas Day and while they were burning it was so festive and beautiful. We were all to-gether and we sang Christmas carols until the candles burnt out, and then it was over. When we still lived at our home back in Peterkau, Christmas was different. There were seldom presents, only a 'Bunten Teller' (a color-ful plate) which was festive and filled with cookies, candies, a few nuts, an apple and a little 'something' hidden on the plate. I remember one Christ-mas in particular, when Mama made and decorated a little Pfefferkuchen Hauschen (gingerbread house) for us. She placed it in the centre of the plate and hid a shiny, sparkling little angel in it for me. It was the most precious gift. Better than the homemade mittens or socks we sometimes got!

In late January 1948, little Herbert had an accident. He went to the kitchen stove and removed the lid from a hot pot of coffee. It tipped and the hot coffee spilled over his stomach, legs and into his shoes. We took his clothing and shoes off as quickly as we could but he was already cov-ered with blisters. We called the doctor who treated the burns with ban-dages and salve. Herbert couldn't walk, so we pushed two chairs together with a pillow on them and there he sat all day long. He played with paper and a pencil and a little toy. Herbert never complained. He was such a good little boy!

When spring arrived, the cattle were able to go outside and there was a lot less work to do in the barn. Our papers to go to Canada were so slow in coming. All during that winter and spring, I became good friends with the kids from the village. It was at this time when I got to know Elizabeth (your Aunt Elizabeth). All the young people used to meet one evening a week in the schoolhouse, and the teacher would play the violin and lead us in singing. Thus, a *Gesangverein* (a choral group) was formed. Ev-ery teenager from the village was there and eventually, some of the older people and married couples attended too. We practised every folk song we knew and we sang in four-part harmony. We never performed anywhere; we just enjoyed getting together and rehearsing. I thought we were pretty good, and it was an evening with something social to do. The dances in the kitchen also continued. Harry often came home on the weekends and it was fun for us all to be together. At this time our everyday life was fairly stable and routine.

Mama had to pay for Harry's board and room. She had to pinch and save to be able to send him to school, where he continued his studies and pharmacy apprenticeship. We sold eggs and cream or whatever we could, even when it meant that at times we didn't eat. In the spring Mama set a hen on some eggs and hatched some chicks. Also, we would get a couple of tiny, little baby pigs from Herr Rosebrock which we fed scraps and raised until they were big enough to butcher for eating. Then Mama sold some of the meat in order to earn more money.

There was one big problem with all of this. Remember all the government regulations I explained earlier? Well, government inspectors would come unannounced and count all the animals people owned. You were only allowed to keep a certain number of animals for yourself and were only allowed a certain amount of meat...the rest was taken away. For example, a family our size was allowed to butcher one pig a year and it had to weigh a certain amount. It was the same with the chickens, geese, ducks or any other animal. The thing that often irritated us was that the British soldiers could come and take any of it and you couldn't do anything about it! I often heard people talking angrily about the fact that all our food went to them! We later learned that the British shipped the provisions back to Great Britain to feed their own starving, suffering people. They tried to make sure that everyone was able to get something to eat... in Germany *and* England.

To combat this problem, our village came up with a well-organized plan. Herr Kaehler, our postman, would get word to us when the government inspector was coming. It was usually very short notice...like just a few hours, but that was enough time for Herr Kaehler to tell Willi, his youngest son, to ride his bike to every house and let them know. When folks heard the news, they stopped working and hurried to hide the animals. We'd put chickens in a sack, run to a field and hide them in a culvert. We had to keep thinking up new ways to hide animals without being caught. I remember one time we had put a pig in the woodshed and piled logs all around him with a lot of food and straw inside with him. The pig was usually quiet. We prayed that the animals would keep silent and often went through some frantic and frightening moments while the inspector was there, because the penalty was terrible for committing this crime. What a relief it was when he was finished and he left! Sometimes we couldn't help laughing afterwards because some people thought of the craziest places to hide their animals. One time, Frau Baumgart, our neighbor, had put her extra pig in her living room (also used as the family's sleeping quarters) with a lot of food. While he was in there, the pig discovered her feather bed and pillows and chewed them all up! That pig had a ball! What a funny sight! There he was lying on the floor in the midst of the remains of the blankets and pillows all covered in feathers! Frau Baumgart didn't think it was so funny!

There were ways and means to have enough food so you wouldn't starve. If you were completely honest and didn't steal, you would have starved to death. Even though the war had ended a couple of years before, food was still scarce. There were, also, ways you could stretch food to make it last longer. I'll tell you about one example. Mama used to boil sugar beets and, then, she'd boil the juice until it became thick syrup. Once it cooled off, we would drizzle it over slices of bread and that would be a meal for our family. We were so hungry…and it tasted so good! It really helped us to be living in the country.

Because we were under the occupation of the British, there was no alcohol allowed anywhere (another regulation). However, there were some people who thought they *had* to have some, so they made their own. My new Papa was one of those people. We found a field with sugar beets. We picked them, cut them up, added water and yeast and let it ferment. (This may have been cooked first, I can't remember.) After it had fermented, they pressed out the liquid, put some of it in a pot that had a jar in the center with a saucer on top of it. They put a lid on the pot and cooked it slowly. The steam formed condensation that dripped into the saucer. This was schnapps. It was potent enough to ignite into flames when put in a spoon and lit with a flame. There were lots of men who were friends that would gather together for an evening of fun that included drinking this 'moonshine.' Making your own alcohol was extremely illegal. The British searched places where they had heard this was happening. When this happened the entire village protected each other. The first person who found out the British were coming sent someone on a bike to let everyone know that they should hide everything. And so it was at our house. One time Mama had a seamstress at our house sewing army clothing into pants and coats. The British were coming to search when we noticed that Papa had overlooked a bottle of schnapps in the kitchen. He grabbed the bottle and said to Frau Janne, "Here…sit on this!" It worked…they didn't find it!

CHAPTER 16
RATZEBURG

We still had not heard any news about our immigration papers. Finally, I had to go back to work to help earn a living. I went to the city of Ratzeburg and found a job as a governess for a widow with five children. She ran a trucking firm and needed someone to care for her children. I enjoyed working for Frau Wulf, but not as much as I had for Frau Blunk. For one thing, I was in the city, and food was very scarce. Only so much food was put on our plates and that was all we got. One thing I did like is that I was able to go home every other Saturday morning until Monday morning. On those weekends I took the bus and walked home to spend precious time with my family.

Ellen and Herbert were growing bigger everyday...Ellen was fourteen months now and Herbert was five years old. I arrived home one weekend in April to find Ellen very sick. She kept getting worse. Mama went to Rosebrock's to phone for a doctor and he came that same night. After examining her, he said she had diphtheria and that she must go to the hospital in Ratzeburg immediately. There was no way we could travel that night. Mama couldn't leave because she was obligated to milk the cows and do the chores. Since I had to return to Frau Wulf's anyway, I told Mama that I'd ride along with the doctor and take Ellen to the hospital. It was the only way.

When we arrived at the hospital and after Ellen was admitted, I was allowed to stay, undress her and put her in the crib. She was burning up with such a high fever. When it was time for me to leave, she was crying and reaching for me. She screamed so hard, I thought my heart would break but, I had to leave her. The tears streamed down my face as I left the hospital and walked across to the other side of town where the Wulf's lived. As I walked along, I couldn't shut out the sound of Ellen's crying in my ears. When I finally arrived at Wulf's, it was three in the morning.

During the following days, I returned to the hospital frequently. The nurses would not allow me to see Ellen. They had such a difficult time calming her down when I left; they felt it was better for her if I did not visit her. I sent daily reports home to Mama about her condition as it was difficult for her to get away from her duties long enough to come to the hospital. Once in awhile she was able to get away long enough to make the trip into town and to the hospital. Later, when Ellen was recovering, I went to the hospital more often and played with her. She didn't cry anymore, so I was allowed to see her every time I visited.

Ellen stayed in hospital for six weeks. When the day finally arrived that we were able to bring her home, I went to the hospital and picked her up. Frau Wulf had given me a few days off from work so I could take her home. She, also, lent me a stroller so I could put Ellen in it as it was a half hour walk from the bus to the village. It had rained and I had to push that stroller over wet ground and around puddles. The ground was so muddy, I really had to struggle. I was so relieved when I got home! I wanted to surprise Mama and Papa. I can still see their faces when I walked into the house with Ellen in my arms. Mama reached for Ellen to kiss and hug her, but, Ellen had been gone a long time and had already forgotten her family…even Mama. Oh, how hurt Mama felt! She wept. It didn't take Ellen long to remember. After she sat on my lap for awhile, she wanted to get down. She ran to the bed, knelt down, looked under it and pulled out the little stool that was kept there. She remembered! Soon she felt right at home and went to Mama. I felt much better by the time I returned to the Wulf's, knowing that Ellen was home and well.

I had been working at the Wulf's for a few months, when, coming home again for the weekend, I found Mama very ill. I went to the barn to help Papa so Mama could stay in bed. When we came in from the barn, we found that Mama had hemorrhaged so badly that blood covered everything. She was having a miscarriage. It really scared me! I ran over to Rosebrock's and they phoned the doctor once more for us. Within an hour Mama was on her way to the hospital. Things looked very bad for her…so much so that the doctors thought she was going to die.

We prayed and pleaded with God to make her well…to save her once more. The Lord heard our prayers. Once more He reached down with His healing hands and made her well. It took a long time before she came home to us again, but we were so thankful that she recovered.

Of course, after Mama went to the hospital there was no question that I must quit my job at Wulf's and return home to help my family. My place now was at home with my brother and sister and I helped Papa in the barn with the milking and all the other chores that Mama had done.

I was seventeen years old now and it was during this time that I became more than good friends with a boy apprentice who worked for Rosebrocks'. His name was George, and he was tall with very blonde, wavy hair. He came from Sachsen and spoke with a Southern German accent. He and his family were refugees and were poor, too. George wanted to be on a farm to learn the trade and be in a place where there was food. He was one of the kindest boys I knew. He would come to the barn and help me by doing all the hard and heavy work I was supposed to do. Whenever and wherever I needed help, he was there to help me. We both enjoyed going for walks and whenever we had an evening free we would take a walk or, he would come over and help me with Herbert and Ellen. He was a marvelous dancer and we did a lot of dancing in Rosebrocks' kitchen.

After two months in the hospital Mama came home. She stayed in bed for a long time. We were so glad she was home again! She looked so terrible…very thin and pale. She couldn't even walk. Whenever she wanted to be up we had to carry her. Mama had a strong will and wouldn't give up…and she finally got well again. I guess God knew we needed her and after all she had been through, it was a blessing to see her strong once again.

And so, everyday life went on. We found Mama's oldest brother and learned that his family had been captured in East Prussia and he was trying to find a way to get them out. That was our Onkel Heinrich. It is so difficult to describe the feeling of joy when a relative was found. We, also, discovered the whereabouts of Tante Elly and her family. We learned they were all well and living in the West Zone. Also, I think it was around this time when Opa became very sick and it was just too difficult for Mama to care for him any longer. He was seventy-five years old now and needed special care. So we had to put him in an "old people's home." The home was in Buechen, which was one and a half hours away by bicycle. We went to visit him on our bikes from time to time. It took most of the day for us to get there, visit and return home again in time to milk the cows. He was always so happy to see us. I really loved my Opa. Opa got a little better, but still needed a lot of daily care. Sometimes he would come home on the weekends if he felt well enough.

In the meantime, the parcels kept coming from Tante Selma and Elsie (in Winnipeg) and Onkel Bill (in Detroit) and were received with such thankful hearts. The dresses that they sent fit me perfectly and I just loved them. They were second hand, but how happy they made me! We, also, received word that our papers were going to take quite some time yet before they would be completely processed. So, I went looking for a job again.

CHAPTER 17
HACKENDORF

I took a position as a governess with a family named Kaestner in Hackendorf. They had two little girls and owned a huge estate. I enjoyed working there. There was enough to eat and we were all treated well. However, we had to be careful as Herr Kaestner was a "ladies' man" and was 'extra nice' to anyone in a skirt. What I liked most about working there was that it was so close to home…only a twenty-minute walk. I could walk home in the evenings after the girls were in bed. Sometimes George would come to meet me and we'd walk home together. We had the most beautiful path to walk on. Anyone who enjoyed nature as much as we did couldn't have missed seeing God's beauty all around them. We were so thankful to be alive!

I had known the people I worked with from an earlier time as we used to socialize together…often just gathering in someone's home for a pleasant evening. I didn't work there very long, however, and I can't even recall why I quit so soon. I think I was only there for about four months. Then, I came home to help Mama, again, for awhile. I think I had quit because I thought our immigration papers were ready…again! But, we still hadn't received them and it seemed like it dragged on forever.

The thought of parting and leaving was so painful, so I was glad the papers weren't ready yet! I had a friend named Helmut Frank from Seedorf who was a baker. After he'd heard that we were leaving soon for Canada, Helmut said, "Of course, if Canada needs bakers, I will come." But you know the old saying 'out of sight, out of mind.' Shortly after we first met at a Fasching (Mardi Gras) dance Mama sent me, by bicycle, to Ratzeburg to do some shopping. On the way, I was to drop a bag of wheat off at the mill (Kogler Muhle) to be made into flour. Well, this happened to be the mill where Helmut worked and somehow he found out that I had brought some wheat in to be ground. When I returned on my bike to pick up the flour, he was standing behind the door waiting for me. He had baked the biggest and prettiest heart shaped cake for me I had ever seen. About ten inches at it's widest! On the way home from the mill, I wondered what to do with the heart, because I didn't want Papa to know about it. I knew Mama wouldn't say anything, but Papa would tease me something terrible and I just couldn't take that. So, I decided to sit down in the ditch and eat it and…that's what I did! After I had eaten it, I cried because it was gone. By the time I got home I was almost sick from eating that huge heart. So, I do have some nice memories from when I was a teenager.

CHAPTER 18
KOLLINGHOF

I had been home for a few weeks when Herr Koeln, the owner of Kollinghof (a large estate) near the neighboring village, asked Mama if I could help out, at his place, for awhile because his wife was expecting twins in the spring. Mama told him I would, and I found myself working again. This is where I met Lotti (the daughter of Mr. Kaehler in Kl-Zecher). She and I did all the house and kitchen work. We were, also, in charge of the chickens. They had such a fancy, new house. We were polishing all the time, and when there wasn't anything to do we had to polish all the doorknobs and clean the windows. This was done every week. We were constantly polishing everything that had silver or brass on it. Lotti and I didn't like working here. The Koeln's were very greedy people. Food wasn't that scarce anymore, but they still divided our meals into small portions and that's all we would get. They kept the cellar and pantry locked at all times. A few times, Lotti and I sneaked a slice of bread out of the pantry under our blouse and ate it later in bed.

About twice a week we walked home. On one of those walks home, we'd get a bunch of sandwiches from Mama and the next time we'd go to the Kaehler's, Lotti's parents, and get some food there. We had a lot of fun on those walks home to get our food supply. We took the food back, hid it in our room and ate it in the evenings. We disliked Herr Koeln so much that we made plans to quit. We did want to stay, though, until the babies were born.

One night at about two in the morning, Herr Koeln knocked on our door and said that they had a baby girl but the second baby died. He told us that he had made previous arrangements with the innkeeper in Gross Zecher, that whenever the babies were born, he would get some wine to celebrate and he told the innkeeper that we would come and get it. We were so shocked that he would even consider sending two young girls out in the middle of the night on such an errand...to walk three kilometres just to get some wine..."WINE!" We weren't even given enough to eat yet he spent money to buy wine! But, we always obeyed orders, especially those coming from Herr Koeln. He was so mean!

Lotti and I got dressed and started out for the innkeeper's place. It was very dark outside as we walked through the forest...we were so scared! To overcome our fear, we sang all the way! We heard all kinds of noises, but our biggest fear was wild boars. We got to the inn and picked up a large bag filled with several bottles of wine. It was so heavy; we had to carry it between us, each of us taking a handle. When we finally got to the top of the hill we looked down and saw the Kollinghof buildings. We were so pooped we decided we would just let them sit and wait awhile for us so we sat down and drank a whole bottle of wine ourselves...besides, we thought, who cares?...there were lots more bottles of wine in there. What fun it was sitting there drinking his wine and imagining them waiting impatiently for us. When we finished our bottle, we resumed our way down the path, singing as we went. We gave Herr Koeln the wine, and to our surprise he wasn't even angry when we told him we had drunk a whole bottle! What a disappointment!!...our joke backfired on us!

It wasn't long after that that I quit because our immigration papers had finally arrived and we were supposed to leave. Then, the full reality of leaving home finally hit me. It was hard to accept the fact that we were going to be leaving everything and everybody we knew. I didn't know any longer if I really wanted to go or not, but Mama kept encouraging us by reminding us of the good opportunities in Canada and how nice it was there. Harry and I finally made the decision to go and were glad because Mama wanted the best for us and she was always right. So...we prepared for our imminent departure.

CHAPTER 19
SAD FAREWELLS

It was now the beginning of May 1949, just before we were to leave for Canada. We decided to visit Tante Elly and family, and also, Onkel Heinrich and his family, who were out of the east zone now. It was the first time we saw any of them since we had fled from the east. It was a marvelous reunion! I shall never forget our trip there and back. We took the train from Luebeck to Hildesheim. We transferred twice, first in Luneburg and, then, in Hanover. It was quite an experience! The trains were so full of people! You couldn't just walk on, you had to push yourself on. First, in Luebeck, the only way we got on was by Harry taking hold of my hand, wriggling himself on and then pulling me on. I thought I was going to be torn apart! People who wanted to get off went through the windows and some even got on the train that way. The closer we got to Hanover the worse it became. People sat or stood on the running boards, on the roof, in the entryways…anywhere and all over. On our way to Hildesheim from Hanover, Harry and I sat on the outside end of a train car where there was a board-like step fastened between cars. We rode like that for fifty kilometres…all the way to Hildesheim.

At Hildesheim we had a very nice visit with everyone. Our cousins, Egbert and Wolfgang, who were our age, were sad that we were leaving to go to Canada. It was like saying goodbye forever. We felt as if we were never going to see each other again, especially since we had only found each other such a short time before. Even though it made us all sad and depressed, I was glad that we had gone to see them.

After we returned home, there were more farewells. Harry's school had a party for him and he invited me to be his table escort. I went to Luebeck to meet him. The faculty from the school had made reservations that evening for us in a Gasthaus along the Elbe River a few kilometres downstream. To get there you had to go by boat...a huge boat that was used to transport people up and down rivers like a bus. Harry's pharmacy class had the whole boat to themselves and it was so much fun! Of course, I didn't know anyone and I felt a little out of place but I still had a marvelous time. At the Gasthaus we had supper and dancing. That was my department! I just loved to dance! There were some good dancers among the guys. (I have a photograph of this party and girls, if you look; it's the one where there is a goat in the picture. Remember?) After this party there was one more weekend of dancing. That was Pentecost. All our friends were there and it was such a sad night filled with mixed feelings... we didn't want the night to end.

One day later in the week, Harry and I rode our bikes to "the old people's home" to see Opa and say goodbye to him. Our hearts were filled with pain because we knew we would never see him on this earth again. This was goodbye forever and I just can't tell you how heavy and sad our hearts were when we left him. I know Opa felt the same way, because he hugged us again and again as he cried. There were so many sad moments we wondered if we would ever be happy again. I did not want to leave.

The last days were spent at home and they flew by quickly. We spent as much time as possible with our family, slowly packing. But what did we have to pack? Harry and I each had one suitcase with some clothing... that's all we had. The time was drawing closer and our hearts grew steadily heavier. Herbert would crawl on my lap and ask questions about us leaving, "Where are you going?" "How quick are you coming back?" "Will you bring me something when you come home?" He asked all these questions with such a sweet innocence. How could we tell him we were never coming home and, maybe, never see him again? In the evenings friends came over and visited. No one was happy. Everyone was sad.

It was June 8, 1949. We had to leave in the morning on the train. Herr Rosebrock said that one of the boys would take us to the station, in Hollenbeck, in the buggy. We stayed up very late the night before we left. Elizabeth came over with a bouquet of flowers for Harry and said goodbye. It didn't ease the pain of leaving.

We hardly slept that night. I know Mama didn't sleep at all. I heard her tossing, turning and weeping all night long. It must have been heart-breaking for her to send her two young children so far away and not know if she'd see them again. I was only seventeen years old and Harry was nineteen. We were up early and got ready to go. Mama made us breakfast. She wanted to come to the station but we wouldn't let her. It would have been too hard to say goodbye there. She agreed. When Karl-Heinz came with the buggy, we put our suitcases on it and, then, it was time to say our final good-byes to Mama. She must have felt so very sad...after all we had gone through and in spite of everything that happened, we managed to stay together through it all and...now we had to part. She wept bitterly, but told us that she knew we would have a better future. To me she said, "You are used to hard work and your brother is not. Stick together no matter what and stand by and help him." To Harry, she said, "All I can say to you is, 'Bete und Arbeite'." That is an old German saying that means if you pray and work all will be fine.

We had kissed Herbert and Ellen goodbye while they slept. It was better for them that they didn't see us leave. Then we were gone. Mama waved and cried. We didn't shed a tear until we were far enough away where she could no longer see us. As we bumped down the road, we kept looking back and saw Mama waving and waving. She waved until we were so far away she was a speck on the horizon. Then, we went around a bend in the road and she and our home were completely out of sight. When Harry and I arrived at the train depot, we both wondered how long Mama had stood waving and we both finally sat down and wept. Afterwards we felt much better. We were headed for a better future and a land where "milk and honey flowed." We began to feel excited. We decided we might as well make the best of it because it is a lot easier to be happy on the outside than to cry and think about the pain of leaving, which was heavy in our hearts.

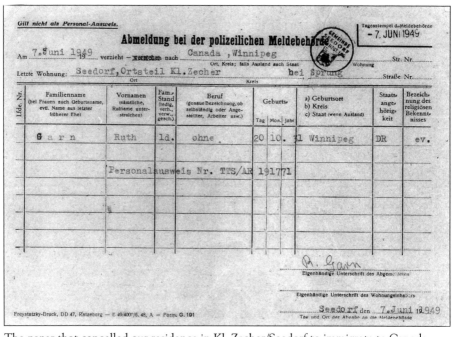

The paper that cancelled our residence in Kl. Zecher/Seedorf to immigrate to Canada.

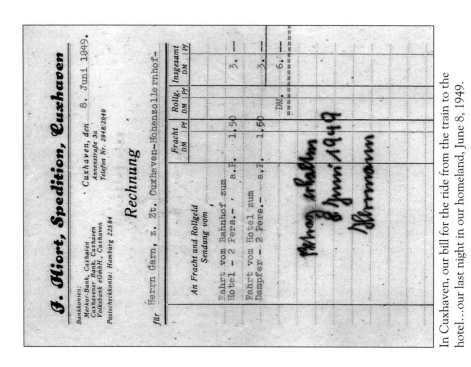

In Cuxhaven, our bill for the ride from the train to the hotel…our last night in our homeland, June 8, 1949.

Our ship, the *Scythia,* carried us from our homeland to Canada.
We were at sea from June 9 to June 20, 1949.

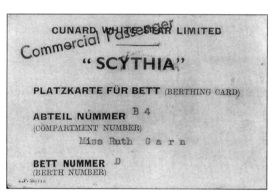

My cabin assignment.

My table assignment.

The Immigration Identifcation card
we received on board ship.

S.S. "SCYTHIA" Sunday, June 19, 1949

LUNCHEON

Potage Albion

Grilled Cod—Maitre d'Hotel

Beefsteak and Kidney Pie

Mixed Vegetables   Mashed and Boiled Potatoes

COLD BUFFET:

Pressed Beef   Oxford Brawn

Salads : Lettuce, Beetroot and Combination

French and Thousand Islands Dressing

Fruit Salad and Custard

Cheese   Biscuits   Coffee

MITTAGESSEN

Dicke Suppe—Albion

Gebratenes Schellfish—Maitre d'Hotel

Beef-shtayk und Nieren Torte

Gemischtes Gemüse

Kartoffel Gekocht   Kartoffelpuree

Kaltes Buffet : Gepresses Beef   Oxford Sulze

SALAT :

Letich, Rote Beeten und Combination—Sauce Pikant

Fruitsalot mit Vanillienkrem

Käse   Biskuit   Kaffee

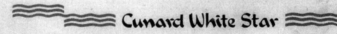

B. 95

A menu from the ship.

The group of young people we had fun with during the journey.

Our travel mates.

A re-union of our relatives in Winnipeg at Art and Lily Garn's farm.

Opa Preuss

Helmut and I were married
on September 29, 1950 at
Lutheran Church of the Cross
in Winnipeg, Manitoba.

This Certifies

That _Helmut Eberhard Werner_
of _Bathgate, North Dakota_
and _Ruth Edith Garn_
of _Winnipeg, Manitoba_
were united in

HOLY MATRIMONY

according to the Ordinance of God
and the Laws of _Manitoba_
at _Winnipeg_
on the _29th_ day of _September_
in the year of our Lord
Nineteen Hundred _Fifty_

Alogh Werner   _Wilfrid K. Betts_
Orma Garl   Pastor

Witnesses

M hither thou
goest, I will go, and
where thou lodgest, I
will lodge: thy people
shall be my people,
and thy GOD my GOD.

Ruth 1:16.

Our wedding invitation.

I received word several weeks after my wedding that Opa Preuss had passed away just two days after Helmut and I were married.

In 1951 Mama sent me this photo of Herbert and Ellen. They were living in Gruenhaus at this time.

Our farm in 1957 in North Dakota. We were replacing the little house with the big one.

Me with my girls in the fall of 1957.

CHAPTER 20
OUR JOURNEY TO CANADA

Harry and I stuck close together. Wherever one was, the other was also. We changed trains in Luebeck and in Hamburg. In Luebeck we knew our way around, but in Hamburg, we had to go to the Canadian consulate to pick up some papers. Here I saw traffic lights for the very first time in my life! I couldn't believe I was in such a big city and it was hard to take it all in. The bombing from the war had been very devastating here and it seemed like there wasn't much left. Later, when our train left the station to go to Cuxhaven, it had to travel through almost the entire city of Hamburg. What an eerie feeling it was to see all the *truemmer* (ruins). It was terrible! We had thought Luebeck was bad, but Hamburg…there were blocks after blocks after blocks…no, kilometre after kilometre…with nothing standing but a chimney here and there and, maybe, parts of some walls. Some places we saw families digging in the ruins. Some were cleaning off bricks. Other places had bulldozers there trying to clean up. This was four years after the war ended! How were they going to clean up all that rubble? Yet, that was the beginning of the rebuilding of Hamburg.

We arrived in Cuxhaven where a bus was waiting to pick us up and take us to the harbour. That's when we discovered that there were a lot of people on that train who were going on the same ship. We noticed them by the travel stickers on their luggage. There was a hotel nearby where we spent the night before going to the ship. That evening Harry and I went to a movie for the last time in Germany. We had some money left over after we paid for all our expenses and couldn't take it along anyway so we decided to spend it on a movie. In the morning we mailed a letter to Mama telling her how things had gone so far and we, also, mailed the rest of our money to her. A bus came again and took us to the pier and our ship. We were so excited!

When we had our first glimpse of that huge ship tied to the pier, we were beside ourselves with excitement! It was huge! There was a lot of standing in lines and checking of papers, but things went along quite smoothly most of the time. When the officers looked at our papers and discovered we were Canadian citizens, they just looked at us, shrugged their shoulders and we didn't have to stand in lines anymore. We could just get on the ship. Of course, we were proud that we didn't have any problems with our papers and were allowed to board.

After we boarded the ship, stewards showed us our rooms. Since this was a British ship they all spoke English. Harry had learned English in school and communicated well enough to get along but, I felt so dumb! I couldn't understand a single word they were saying so I just looked all around and I loved what I saw! Everything was so beautiful! This was one of the nicer ocean liners. Our cousin and Onkel had given us tickets in Class B, which isn't as elaborate as Class A, but to us it was like heaven! It scared me terribly when Harry and I had to stay on separate sides of the ship. I had a room on the women's side and he was on the men's side. I was so afraid, if I got lost, Harry would never find me. My cabin consisted of three rooms, but since there were so many people I had to share my cabin. I had a room in my cabin, way in the back, all by myself. There was a lady with three children in the front rooms and they spoke German. How happy I was to not be all alone!

After everyone was checked in and on board, everyone had to report to their stewards. From them we each got cards...one for our rooms and one for the dining room. Our room numbers and the decks they were located on were written on them and we had to carry them at all times, so, in case someone got lost they could help us get back to where we belonged.

Late that afternoon the ropes to the dock were untied and we pulled away from the dock. It was very interesting watching them raise the bridge, and those little tugboats pulling that giant monster into deep water. I don't think I ever saw so many people in one place before! There were 2,000 passengers on board and twice that many on shore waving. Everyone waved, even those who didn't have family or friends on shore to wave to. We did, too. You waved because you were leaving…leaving the land and the people you loved…leaving our beloved homeland! Those people on shore represented all of our loved ones and all that we loved and were leaving. Harry ran to his cabin and brought back our accordion which Mama and Papa had given us as a farewell gift (don't know how they managed to buy that). He came back and started playing, *"Nun Ade du Mein Lieb Heimat-land"* (Farewell to My Beloved Homeland), I started singing and suddenly lots of other passengers began singing along. A man began playing another accordion just like ours (except his was blue and ours was red) and we sang and cried until our beloved homeland was a line on the horizon.

Soon it was time for our first meal aboard and we had to find our way to the dining room and to our table. I couldn't believe all the food! There was a menu, not to choose from, but to tell you about all the foods you were going to be eating! A lot of the food I had never heard of before. Like toast…what was that? And so, I had my first toast in my life aboard that ship. There were three courses of food. I just couldn't believe it!! Was this really happening to us? There were eight people at our table. Plates of buns and toast and other things were set on the table and you could eat as much as you wanted. When other people were through taking what they wanted, I usually took what was left because I wasn't going to let any food be taken back from our table! After that first supper we had a safety drill with swim vests and had instructions as to what to do in order to save our lives in case the ship would sink. We were all assigned to certain lifeboats and the procedures connected with them were explained to us. After that we were free to do as we liked.

We decided to explore the ship. At least we tried but it was just too big to see all of it. We made a lot of friends, though, in the process. Most of them were travelling alone and, also, headed for a better future in Canada. There were about ten or eleven of us who became good friends and stuck together every day.

Our first day out Harry and I were called to the Purser's Office and we each received $8.00. Onkel Bill and our cousin Art had sent it to us for spending money. We were so happy about that. They had many gift shops on board and we bought little things like a pen or a comb with the ship on it. We bought postcards of the ship and stamps to mail back to Mama. We had such great times on that big floating city. There was every sort of game to play that you could ever think of…like tennis, table tennis, swimming and all kinds of other things to do, too. We felt like we were living in the movies! We met a couple of Danish fellows, who were just great, only we couldn't communicate with them. The only way we could communicate was through Harry talking with them in the little English he knew. The next day the ship docked in Le Havre, France, to pick up more 'refugee' passengers. Harry and I had so much fun watching the ship dock and leave again. Fascinating!

Almost every night we would go on the upper decks and play catch. There were thirteen of us now and we hung out together and had the most unforgettable fun. Sometimes we would stand at the stern of the ship and just watch the water. Phosphorous[21] would light up the bubbles coming out of the exhaust from the boat in the water. The bubbles glowed in a stream that was twenty metres long or more. It was mesmerizing. The nights were difficult, though, because it was then, that we felt lonely and homesick for our home and family. I dreaded going to bed. The happier days made up for it.

On the fourth day at sea, we were hit by a storm that lasted for three days. It was terrible! All the upper decks were closed because the waves washed right over them. Out of our portholes we could see the wild ocean outside. It looked like huge mountains with the ship going, first, up one side and then down the other. We thought it was going to be the end of us because it seemed to go on and on. Many people were seasick and Harry was one of them. On the first day of the storm, there were four of us at our dining table. Then, Harry and another person became ill, and there were just two of us left. I made up my mind that I was *not* going to get sick. What a blessing it was to wake up on the fourth morning and find calm seas. It was good to sleep without getting thrown around. Slowly, after that, people began to recover, although many were still quite pale. We gathered with our friends again and enjoyed many hours together, going to movies and dancing, etc.

On the tenth day we were told we would soon see land. We stood for three hours that afternoon at the railing watching the horizon for a tiny line that would indicate land. Finally, someone saw something out there and the shouting started. People jumped and laughed and hugged each other because they were so happy to see land. But it took all that night and most of the next day before we got close enough to actually see things on shore. Many of the people stood by the railing most of the time. All we saw were very high and straight cliffs with lots of trees. We saw no signs of habitation. Some of the cliffs were almost white. It was interesting to watch the shoreline going by, since we had never seen any land quite like this before.

CHAPTER 21
CANADA

On June 20, 1949 we landed in Quebec, Canada. We watched, fascinated once again, as the tugboats towed our ship in, the bridges being raised and lowered for us and, finally, maneuvering the ship to the docks by the tugboats. By the time our ship was tied to the docks it was late in the afternoon. Harry and I and a few others, who were also Canadian citizens, were allowed to go ashore. No one else was allowed to leave as they had to go through immigration first and the immigration office had already closed for the day. There wasn't much of a town along the harbour. It was almost open country. Harry and I went for a walk along some roads close by and I picked my first flowers from this new land (I still have those flowers, which I pressed in a book, to this day). We only had about half an hour to walk around before we had to return to the ship for our last meal on board.

That night we had a farewell party. We went to the dance on board ship, but it meant saying goodbye to all the friends we had made during the journey. The next day, everyone went in different directions. Most of them took the CPR (Canadian Pacific Railway) to the places they were going. However, Harry and I and an older man named Mr. Belter, were to board the CNR (Canadian National Railway), which was supposed to be better, but we would have preferred to travel with our friends. We had to be at the CNR station at noon to catch our train to Winnipeg. Harry went to get the train tickets, which we thought had been paid for by Art and

Uncle Bill and would be waiting for us. Harry soon came back and said we still owed $8.00 towards those tickets. I was so scared, "What are we going to do?" I cried, "We shouldn't have spent any money on board the ship and then we would have been fine!" "But, that was supposed to be pocket money for us on board," Harry said, "How much do you have left? Let's count all we have."

We put all our money together and between us were able to come up with the $8.00. That left us with only $0.50 for both of us for the rest of our trip. We didn't worry, because we thought we would be there soon. Do you know how far it is from Quebec to Winnipeg? I never knew of a land that could be that big! We travelled the rest of that day, all that night, all the next day and all the next night. The day after that, on June 23rd, we finally arrived in Winnipeg at 11:00 a.m. Can you imagine making $0.50 stretch that far? We did it! After all the food we had aboard the ship, we had to go hungry again. We couldn't buy a pillow to sleep on, which wasn't that important, but the food…We watched others eat. We would press our face against the window watching people walk around the stations with ice cream cones and wondering what our future would be like in this new land.   I couldn't speak English and it was so hot here! We drank a lot of water. The train went through Montreal at night and I couldn't believe all the lights especially after all the darkness we experienced in Germany. I couldn't understand why so many lights were burning for no reason and so many kinds of signs going off and on in all colors of the rainbow. Some were shaped like stars, arrows and, even, words! I couldn't believe it! I just stared at it all!

CHAPTER 22
WINNIPEG, MANITOBA

When we arrived in Winnipeg, our stomachs were in knots from hunger. We got off the train and stood there on the platform not knowing what to do next. We didn't know anyone, but we were told that our relatives were notified of our arrival. We wondered how we would recognize them. Soon, everyone had left, even the train. There we stood…just the two of us with our two suitcases. We thought, "This is the land where milk and honey flows?" We were hungry, tired and alone…Harry with his limited English and me, who couldn't speak a word.

Because we didn't know what else to do, we decided to wait awhile longer. Soon two people came up the steps and asked if we were Harry and Ruth. We both said, "Yes!" and they said, "We are Art and Lili Garn, your cousins." We were so happy to see them, but I sure felt a terrible pang of disappointment in my heart. I looked in the direction from where they had come. No one else had come to meet us…just Art and Lili. That was all. Another man was supposed to be there, but I couldn't see him anywhere. I guess, in the back of my mind, I had actually come to believe that our Papa would be there. Because he was a Canadian citizen, I had talked myself into believing that he came here right after the war was over and was unable to get in touch with us. Down deep, I just knew he would meet us at the station. Then, I thought, maybe he didn't come along… maybe he was at the house. After all this time, I hadn't accepted the fact my Papa was dead.

Art and Lili helped us with the suitcases and we left the station for the parking lot. I was surprised to see everything so big...and such wide streets! I couldn't imagine why they would have such wide streets. What a waste of space! We drove with Art and Lili to Alma and Gus Lorentz's house on Alexander Avenue (Alma is my cousin and Art's sister). They had a hot meal ready for us and what a feast it was! We could eat as much as we wanted and...we did! It tasted marvelous! I was still disappointed that Papa wasn't there. It took me a long time to accept the fact that Papa must have died.

That same evening we left Gus and Alma's house and went to Art and Lili's farm. I loved it there and accepted it as my new home. It took awhile, of course, to get used to everything being so big...big gardens, big yards, big fields and big roads. I couldn't believe how much land was wasted. There were actually corners and whole parts of the yard that were never put to productive use.

On our first Sunday on the farm, Harry and I met all our uncles and aunts, cousins, cousins-in-law and their children. Everyone spoke excellent German except the children. After that we tried to familiarize ourselves with the Canadian way of life and we helped whenever we could. Harry worked in the field almost every day and to him it was exciting to drive the tractor and truck. I helped in the house and garden and did the chores alone. But, whenever, there was time, I went to a quarry that was in their pasture and cried my heart out with homesickness.

Art and Lili had two little girls. Doreen was four years old and Linda was nine months old. Doreen didn't like me very well. She couldn't understand what I was saying, but I soon spoiled Linda. I carried her everywhere. I walked her to sleep. I carried her morning, noon and night. I thought of Herbert and Ellen and covered Linda with kisses instead. The evenings were the most depressing. Quite often, Harry looked for me and always found me sitting at the edge of the quarry sobbing. It was always worse when a letter came from Mama or one of our friends back home. It took five weeks for a letter to arrive from Germany and, of course, phone calls were impossible. Air mail was not affordable and often not available.

After a couple of months, Harry and I decided it was time to make plans for our future. Harry's fare would soon be paid off through our labour. Gus and Alma told us that their two-room apartment would be vacant by the first of October and we could rent it if we wanted it. We took it.

CHAPTER 23
SURVIVING IN WINNIPEG

We moved in and owed them our first month's rent of $30.00. Alma, also, bought some dishes and other items for us to set up housekeeping with. We paid them back in installments of $2.00 each week. We both had jobs now. Harry worked on a cutting table in a sewing factory where they made fur coats. I worked in the same building, but for a different company, making pants, jackets and western shirts. I operated a buttonhole machine and a button machine. Both of us made $0.45 per hour. We walked to and from work because we couldn't afford to ride the bus. We couldn't even afford to eat very well. After paying rent and other payments, there wasn't much left. We needed new clothes because we had gained a lot of weight with the climate and food changes, but, we just got the most necessary items. We wanted to send a package home for Christmas and by saving every little bit we managed to send them something.

We made some new friends and they gave us some clothing. Harry met a fellow at work who was German and had just come over from Kiel, Germany, the year before. His name was Karl Rangno. He became such a good friend and he could speak English fairly well, so he often helped us. Whenever we went out, the three of us went together. We went to dances and movies and had lots of fun together. There were only two places to dance. One was at the Ukrainian Hall and the other was the Barn dance. The Barn dance was all western music and it fascinated us. At the Ukrainian Hall it was all German music and dancing. We made a lot of friends there. There was, also, a German Hall, but it only held dances on special weekends. One weekend we went to a masquerade dance there. Uncle Harry dressed up as a cowboy and I dressed up as a *Coca Cola* queen. I fastened *Coca Cola* caps all over a long dress. I made a red crown with *Coca Cola* caps all over it. To fasten the caps, I made two holes in the center of a cap and sewed it on like a button. It turned out wonderful!

Now I must tell you a funny story about myself. My favorite food in this new land was ice cream. I had never tasted such good, creamy ice cream. Before we left Germany, you could get ice cream too, but it was made with frozen water. So every penny I saved that was extra, I spent on ice cream. One hot day I walked home from work all alone as Harry had gone home early because business was slow at his work. I wanted an ice cream cone so badly I could taste it but I still couldn't speak English and Harry wasn't with me to help me buy it. After walking a few more blocks, I gathered up enough courage to go in a place that sold ice cream. I thought that if I said, "ice cream," they would know what I wanted. But instead, he asked me something in return and I couldn't understand what it was. I just repeated one of the words he had said to me hoping I had said the right thing. Well, it turned out I didn't. He gave me a half-gallon of ice cream in a paper bag. Not knowing what else to do, I held up a handful of change and he took what he needed. How could I explain I didn't want a half-gallon of ice cream? That all I wanted was a cone? So, I took it and went home. When I got there, Harry was already gone to a night school class that he had joined to learn to speak English. Here I was with this box of ice cream! *Want to know what I had for supper?* Yup! Ice cream! We had no refrigerator. I spooned away at that ice cream until I thought I would be sick at any moment. I finally put some away until Harry came home, but, of course, it melted.

Our, or I should say, *my* homesickness continued. I was so homesick I was physically ill…especially on those evenings and Sundays when the German hour was on the radio. Those were the times I wept until my eyes burned and there were no more tears left. Then, one day, a letter came from Mama asking us to save our money and come home. They missed us so much. But how could we save anything making $0.45 an hour? We could hardly live on that! How could we save enough to go home? It hurt so much, wanting to go home and not being able to do so. Karl suggested we try to have them come to Canada. So we wrote and asked. They said, 'Yes, but how?" That took money, too.

We lived from one day to another. Harry decided to try to get into his field of work, which was pharmacy. But, he couldn't afford to go to university so when a job in a drugstore opened up, he thought that if he could get it, maybe he could work his way into a better position. He asked what I thought and I said okay. The job only paid $10.00 per week but, we were willing to try it.

We joined Luther League and choir at the Church of the Cross, which was a Lutheran church next door to us. All of our relatives attended this church, too. I, also, joined the Sunday school staff and taught a class in German to fourteen children from ages six to fourteen. This filled a lot of my free time and the Lord took care of my homesickness and aching heart.

Throughout the following winter, we just weren't able to live on Harry's reduced salary at his new job so he was forced to look for a different job. Jobs were difficult to get at this time. Harry answered an ad for a door-to-door salesman with the Paula Company. (This company was a lot like the Watkins Company that sold spices, etc.) He bought the case that held all the little samples. He said he would be able to make "big bucks." It was difficult with no car and speaking broken English. He didn't even make enough to pay for the sample case and after three weeks he knew he would starve on the money he made. He began searching for another job. He saw an ad in the paper looking for a bookkeeper for a food service company in Shilo, Manitoba; he applied and got the job. Then we realized that he would have to leave town, because Shilo was two hundred kilometres away from Winnipeg but, he still decided to take the job and left. Now here I was, all alone in my loneliness.

By this time we had become good friends with the Weiss family who lived across the street. Their daughter, Helga, was in my Sunday school class. Alvine Weiss was alone a lot, too, as her husband was a carpenter and had to be out of town throughout the week building houses with different companies. We were two lonely hearts together...Alvine and me. We ate supper at her house and walked to and from work together. They had come from Germany, too, so we talked a lot about our homeland. We spent a lot of time together.

In February of 1950, I met a man that my cousin, Art, knew. He was a nephew of Art and Lili's neighbor, Auntie Olga. One evening, Auntie Olga came over to Alma's and called upstairs for me to come down. When I did, she said, "Ruth, I want you to meet my niece and nephew, Renata and Helmut Werner, from the States." I barely looked at them and said, "How do you do?" and ran back upstairs. Doreen Kroll, who had come with them, came upstairs and asked if I wanted to join them for a movie... and I did. It was a bitterly cold and snowy evening. I couldn't understand enough English to follow the story in the movie. Also, this guy, Helmut, had parked his car in a 'no parking' zone. When we got out of the movie theatre he had received a parking ticket and he was in a very bad mood and said nasty things. He scared me. I was glad to, eventually, be back in my cozy little room. There wasn't anything enjoyable about the evening.

That spring, Karl came by often to help me work on the immigration papers to bring my family over from Germany but, we could only go so far with the applications since we didn't have the money to pay for their trip. Harry sent me a little money here and there so I could keep both rooms of the apartment so when he came home on the weekends he had a place to sleep.

CHAPTER 24
NORTH DAKOTA

One day I received a letter from the guy I had met in February who was from the States. Helmut asked me to write to him. I could hardly speak never mind write! I waited until one weekend when Harry was home and I asked him to write a letter for me, then, I copied it. And that, girls, is how the romance started between your father and me. Helmut came to visit twice that summer and in July we were engaged to be married. I was eighteen years old. When Karl found out I was engaged, he came over and gave me a stern lecture on why I would do such a thing…especially after only seeing this man a few times! "Besides," he said, "Here I am and why do you think I was so interested in you and your family and trying to help you?" But, even then I was still dumb and said, "Yes, I know, Karl. You are a good friend."

Later, when Helmut and I got married on September 29, 1950, I found out what Karl's intentions had been and that he really loved me. He was a designer of fur coats and worked for the company where Harry had his first job. I knew he had a good future in life and would do well. But, my heart was with Helmut and in the country…on the farm…*where there would <u>never</u> be a shortage of food.*

After our marriage, I moved to Bathgate, North Dakota where Helmut's farm was located. Once again I had to go through the whole business of immigration papers and a lot of 'red tape', because I had lived in Germany most of my life. But, I was able to move to North Dakota on a visa. Here on our farm I made a little world of my own. I didn't know a single soul. I had only met Ed and Alvina twice and Uncle Alex and Auntie Delma once (Daddy's brother and sister-in-law and his aunt and uncle). They were people who were born here and I knew they could never know how it felt to have my family and my homeland so far away. Even Harry was far away now. He was the only one here who mattered to me and I couldn't see or talk to him either. Then, he was promoted to supervisor of food services for Crawley McCracken (a food service company that contracts out to various companies to feed workers) in Sheridan, Manitoba which was way up north and farther away yet.

We had been married for about a week when I received a letter from Mama telling me that my beloved Opa had passed away on October 1st. His death was only two days after our wedding. Mama wrote that on the last day he was alive, he kept calling my name, but there was no way to get in touch with me. That hurt me so much. To know he called me in his last hours and I couldn't be with him. But I said, "Thank you, Lord that Mama was able to be with him." Opa was seventy-seven years old and died of liver cancer.

The first winter of our marriage I was so lonely. We lived in a tiny two-room house and, I mean tiny…it was only 12 by 20 foot…that's 240 square feet. Can you imagine? The house had no electricity or running water. We used to buy ice blocks, split them and melt them on the stove for water, which was a lot better than melting snow. We had to place straw bales all around the bottom of the outside of the house to keep the cold from coming through the walls and foundation. To pass the time during the evenings, I did a lot of sewing and knitting by lamplight. Then I discovered during the winter that I was going to have a baby! That seemed so wonderful to me. Now, I would have something that would be my very own.

Spring finally came and I was excited to be doing things outdoors. I set hens on nests and hatched my own little chicks instead of buying them. We bought some geese and duck eggs and I set hens on them to hatch them, too. I had a garden. I was in my glory with that big garden! I planted it and watched it grow. All this, too, belonged to me. I could scarcely believe it! I kept digging all over the place planting things here and there trying to make things look nice but, soon I gave up and learned the American way of wasting land and space because I just couldn't plant it all. I was happy. I was so wrapped up in my world and work.

On July 12, 1951, we had a baby girl. She weighed eight pounds, six ounces and we named her Edith Marie. I was so happy! I know the new father would have liked to have had a son, but there wasn't much we could do about it. She was so cute with blue eyes and black hair.

It was a terrible summer with all the outside work and caring for a new baby. I had a difficult time dealing with the hot weather plus we had to keep the fire in the stove burning all the time for cooking and canning. The heat in our little house was unbearable. In the summertime we got our water from the Tongue River which flowed through our farm about one hundred yards from the house. When I had to carry all the water indoors that I needed for laundry, cleaning and cooking, those one hundred yards seemed more like a mile But, I was accustomed to hard work and didn't mind. It never occurred to me to ask why there was no electricity or running water until two years later when another baby arrived.

CHAPTER 25
MY FAMILY ARRIVES IN WINNIPEG

When my first baby was born, I wrote to Mama and told her that she had become a Grandma. She felt so sad that she couldn't be with us and see her first grandchild. She wrote and asked, again, if there was some way to help them come over but it was even more difficult to get them into the United States. We went to Winnipeg and filled out affidavits and other immigration papers, there was still no word from the immigration office. Mama decided to see if she could get immigration papers in Germany that would help them get over here. They were able to do it this time, but they still had to wait until they could pay their fare. Finally, in July of 1952, we received a telegram saying that Mama, Papa, Herbert and Ellen were going to arrive in Winnipeg. It all happened so fast that Mama didn't even have time to write us a letter. Oh, you can't imagine how happy I was! On Tuesday, July 15, 1952, three days after Edith's first birthday, we drove to Winnipeg to meet them at the train station. Harry came down from Sheridan, too. We left our farm early for the two hour drive to Winnipeg. We arrived at the station early; to be sure we'd be on time to meet the train. When I first glimpsed the coming train, tears started flowing down my cheeks. I began to wonder what they would look like. Would they still be the same? Would Herbert and Ellen still know me? And would they *really* be on that train?

The train came to a stop and passengers started to get off. We looked at every person and then, there they were, all four of them, dressed so nicely…and we flew into each other's arms, weeping with joy. Herbert and Ellen kept staring at us. I don't think they remembered us very well. Herbert may have remembered us a little bit more since he was six years old when we left but Ellen was a little shy. Of course, she was only two years old when we left Germany and three years had gone by since then. She was so sweet; I just wanted to squeeze her.

We drove to Alma and Gus's home where they had prepared a wonderful meal for all of us. In the afternoon, Mama, Papa, Harry and I went for a walk around the neighbourhood. Mama could still remember most of the streets. We looked for places to rent. As we walked down Pacific Avenue, we saw a sign in the window, "Apartment for Rent." We stopped and looked at it. Mama said that it was fine for their first home. She, also, told me that it was only a few houses away from the house where I was born. I was so excited and asked her to show it to me.

Later in the afternoon we went to Art and Lily's farm. Mama wanted to see if it had changed since they had left. We had a nice visit there and spent the night with them. The next morning Harry bought some cheap furniture for Mama and Papa…a dining room set and bedroom set…and moved them into their apartment. Some of the relatives gave them pieces of furniture to use, as well. By the end of the next day they were all moved in and Helmut and I had to get back to the farm. Harry stayed with them a little longer and helped them get more settled in. Mama and Papa found jobs right away; Papa at a factory making chrome furniture and Mama working nights as a cleaning lady at the phone company. The children adjusted to the English language quickly, started school in September and made new friends but Ellen still asked, "When are we going home?"

After we had our work on the farm 'caught up', Edith and I returned to Winnipeg and stayed with Mama for a week. It felt strange to go to Winnipeg to visit them. How wonderful it was to see them and not have that big ocean between us any longer. We had such a wonderful time together and Mama loved her little grand-daughter to bits. Soon it was time for Edith and I to return to the farm but, that was okay because we knew they were not so far away now. We couldn't chat on the phone daily like folks do these days as there were no phone lines in our area yet. Later, with all of the harvest and fall work on the farm, we weren't able to visit them as much as we would have liked.

CHAPTER 26
SURVIVING ON THE FARM

With the arrival of every fall came butchering time...but this time it brought tragedy. We butchered a hog and when we were preparing the meat and making sausage, Edith, who was just sixteen months old, was badly burned. It was partially due to my carelessness. I had been simmering sausages in a large pressure cooker and had just removed it from the stove and set it on the floor so I could take the sausages out (remember we had a tiny kitchen). Edith was standing in the kitchen and Helmut was playing with her when she backed up and fell into it. It was full of hot water and melted lard. Her back, bottom and upper legs were burned so badly that when we took her clothing off, her skin came off, too. We wrapped her in a sheet and blanket and took her to the hospital in Altona, Manitoba. It was twenty miles away and the nearest hospital at that time. They bandaged her burns and sent us home. We were instructed to leave the bandages on her undisturbed, for ten days and then bring her back. Edith was so lethargic and just lay in her bed...after a few days her condition deteriorated. Her injuries started to smell so I loosened a bandage to peek at the burns. I found the injuries covered with yellow pus and she, also, had a temperature. We took her back to the hospital immediately. By this time five days had passed and a different doctor examined her. He told us her burns were infected and she would have to be hospitalized. I was so upset and I told them so. What a dumb way of doing things! She stayed in the hospital for a whole week and I made sure she was healing properly before we took her home again. Some of the burns that were very deep had to be bandaged for a long time but I was able to change the bandages at home. What a terrifying time!

The winter of 1952 was rapidly approaching. It was fun to get everything 'rounded up' for winter in North Dakota and fall was always a busy time preparing for the long winter season. We dug a hole under our little house so we could store our canned food, potatoes and other vegetables. Opening a little trap door in the floor was a lot easier than going to the barn to get food and it kept a lot better, too. We butchered our own pigs and canned most of the meat. Some of it we kept in a freezer locker in Cavalier but I liked having food stored at home since it wasn't unusual to be stormed in for a week or two at a time.

It was during this time that I discovered we were going to have another baby. This child, too, would be born in the summer. This was our third winter on the farm and it was much better. We still only had two little rooms in our house but it didn't matter so much. The hardest part was thinking about another baby coming with still no electricity or water. Folks living near us had them already. I began to question "Why?" "How come?" "What can we do?" "How much money would it cost?" I thought we could go without some extras and try to save money, but I learned that the R.E.A. (Rural Electric Association) was not allowed to put electrical poles in the ditches because when the roads needed to be graded the poles were in the way. And there were other problems. Before even getting to our property, poles would have to be placed across a neighbor's land and they, of course, wouldn't allow it. And even if we were able to get the lines to our property, they would have had to cut across our farmland diagonally, making a lot of the land unusable. Your Dad didn't want to do that either. We went through a lot of letter writing and court hearings which all seemed so senseless to me. I just couldn't believe that there were people who would deny others a good and necessary thing like electricity, so we lived through another winter in our little house with kerosene lamps for light and melting ice for water. I didn't really mind though, because that's the way country life is...in *my* mind anyway. There were some improvements coming though.

The summer of 1953 was as hot as the summers before it but this time we set up a kerosene stove in the garage so the house would stay cooler. I wouldn't have set it up in the house anyway as it smoked so badly all my kettles turned black with soot but it washed off easily. This little stove even had a small oven which you could set on top and I could bake bread and cakes. Having the stove in the garage helped lessen one of my hardships...cooking in the hot, hot house.

The worst hardship was washing clothes. With another baby coming, I would have lots of extra clothing and diapers to wash and I dreaded having to carry all that water so far again. After much pleading, Daddy finally bought a stock tank.[22] He put it on a stoneboat[23] and pulled it with the tractor to the river, filled it with water and pulled it back to the house where it sat. Oh my, I was so happy!! No more carrying water from the river!! I would just go outside the house to the tank and scoop up water for washing. But, as with all good things, there were drawbacks. I was so afraid that Edith would play there, fall in and drown. We had a cover made for it but, even then, there was still some danger of falling in. I'll never forget, once I heard Edith crying outside. I ran out to see what happened. Here she came from the direction of the stock tank with blood running down her face and hair. I was choked up with fear, thinking, "What happened?" It turned out that she had bumped her head on a bolt that was sticking out from underneath the truck.

From time to time we went to Winnipeg to be with Mama and Papa and each time it was a wonderful reunion. During the winter it was more difficult to go. Both Mama and Papa were doing well at their jobs. They sure knew how to save money and just before Christmas they bought a house. It was an old house but now they had a home of their own. Their house had three bedrooms and a bathroom upstairs and a kitchen, dining room and living room downstairs. There was a closed veranda on the front and a storage room and entry in the back. They rented all the bedrooms to German people who had just immigrated. In one room were Walter and Frieda. The second room had Karl Heinz and in the third was Klaus. They converted the dining room into a bedroom for themselves and Herb and Ellen. The renters shared the refrigerator, stove and bathroom with Mama and Papa without any problems. They were all so happy and thankful to have so much. Mama and Papa had many German friends, so they didn't have to fight homesickness like I did. Of course, we weren't living too far apart and that helped a lot.

On one of our visits to Winnipeg, Mama told me a very exciting story:

> One day she was on her way to work at the telephone company. She always took the streetcar downtown and, then, walked a couple of blocks to the building she worked in. She was standing on the corner of Portage and Main waiting for a green light. A man was standing near her and kept looking at her…she began to feel uncomfortable. He came closer to her and asked, "Are you Mrs. Garn from Germany?" She said, "Yes, I _was_ Mrs. Garn, but I am Mrs. Sprung now." He, then, said, "Do you remember me? I'm the soldier who was at the gate. I'm the guard from the base at Blankensee. You brought your little boy there." Mama was speechless. The light changed from red to green many times while they stood there and talked, exchanging addresses and phone numbers. We were reunited with our angel…what a miracle!

Harry was still working for Crawley McCracken and was first stationed in Edmonton, Alberta, then in Sheridan, Manitoba and later in Churchill, Manitoba. It was a long way from Winnipeg so he didn't get home very often, but when he did we would always get together and spend time reminiscing. Mama thought it was time for Harry to get married and settle down closer to Winnipeg. Harry said, "I have been writing to Elizabeth for four years and if I get married, I'll send for her." Mama said, "Why don't you? What are you waiting for?" So Harry did the paperwork required to bring Elizabeth over from Germany. I suppose she was shocked, too, that it all finally happened. I guess it was pretty awkward and funny when Harry went to meet Elizabeth at the train station because he had bought a big bouquet of flowers and wanted to meet her alone…but Mama came along. I guess he arranged for Mama to stand somewhere else so his first meeting with her could be somewhat alone! They had to start planning their wedding immediately as immigration laws required that they marry within one month after her arrival.

I was sorry I couldn't be in Winnipeg to share their joyous reunion, but I had just given birth to another baby girl, Karen Diane, on July 9, 1953, weighing seven pounds, twelve ounces. I had meant to spell her name K-a-r-i-n, but didn't know that in this country they spelled it with an 'e', which is what they put on her birth certificate. Rather than create a fuss, I left it as it was. But, I kept on spelling it my own way. Karin had really dark hair, a dark complexion and the brownest eyes anyone had ever seen. She, like Edith, was born in Drayton, North Dakota assisted by Dr. Waldren. He was a big, husky man who seemed to know his work very well (sadly, two years later he committed suicide by shooting himself.)

After five days in the hospital, I went home with our new little girl. Edith wouldn't leave my side. While I was in the hospital she stayed with Ed and Alvina in the day and with Daddy in the evenings and nights. She was so happy to have me and her new baby sister at home. I was still very weak from childbirth and tried not to do too much, but there was so much work that had to be done. It was summer time and the flies were such a problem. It was difficult to keep them out of the house. As soon as one came in I tried to kill it right away. I shouldn't have done that because when I stretched to hit a fly on the ceiling…I began hemorrhaging. We had to get to the hospital right away. We had a huge problem getting there though. We lived 1¾ mile from Highway 18 which was a gravel road. The road that went past our farm was dirt. It had been raining for two days straight which made the road muddy and the black mud was like gumbo. As we drove, the mud kept sticking to the tires. The wheels were getting bigger and bigger until they couldn't turn anymore. A neighbor came with his tractor and pulled us all the way to Highway 18, but the gravel was in terrible shape…with deep ruts and impossible to drive on. So our neighbor pulled us all the way to Highway 5, which was blacktop. Then we took off as fast as we could. I thought that I was going to bleed to death and leave behind my two little girls. I ended up back in the hospital for another five days and Karin stayed with me as I was nursing her. Edith spent the days, again, with Ed and Alvina. When I returned home the second time, everything went well.

Daddy decided to do some improvements on the house. He wanted to build a short addition, maybe four or five feet long, onto the house that could be used as a mudroom. He figured it would be the easiest way to keep the cold from coming directly into the house plus we could keep our boots, coal pail and other "outside" stuff in there. Daddy, also, thought if he built it the full twelve foot width of the house it would be even better. However, since all the lumber he bought was already eight feet long he decided to make it that long. I was so thrilled! In my mind I was thinking what a cute kitchen that 8 by 12 foot room would make! After he was finished building I told him what I had been thinking and I asked him to help me move everything from the old kitchen into the "new" kitchen. He couldn't believe it. He said he built a mudroom not a kitchen. I said, "Oh, you just thought you did. No room that size is going to be used as a mudroom!" So, now we had a kitchen...and a living room in the middle. Now I was living first class! We got a couch, a picture (which is still, to this day, hanging over the couch downstairs in my house) and oh, I was so happy arranging things! Now I had a house where I could go from one room to another...and remember, now the house was a lot bigger at 336 square feet!!

Mama was so anxious to visit us, to see where we lived and what it was like around our area, but they still couldn't cross the border. They had to stay in Canada for five years without leaving in order for them to become Canadian citizens. After that, they would be allowed to cross the border. We had made a date to meet one Sunday in Gretna, a little town just on the other side of the border. I packed a picnic lunch with fried chicken and we drove to Gretna, which was only ten miles away from our farm. Mama, Papa, Herb and Ellen traveled there and back by bus. We found a nice spot to have our picnic together. We drove along the border and showed them the direction we lived and they seemed happier just knowing approximately where we were located. Shortly after this, to our surprise, they started the paperwork required to apply for permanent residence in the United States. It made me so happy. Mama wanted us all to live in the same country. She knew if they came, Harry would probably come sometime, too.

Harry and Elizabeth were married August 14, 1953. Karin was only four weeks old and I was still quite weak but we still went to Winnipeg for the wedding. They had such a beautiful wedding. It meant so much for our family to be together but, of course, Elizabeth was sad because none of her family could be there. I knew how she felt because I had gone through the same experience. We had known her for so long and loved her so much. Because Elizabeth and I had been close friends since we were teenagers in Germany so we could talk about anything and everything together. Harry and Elizabeth spent part of their honeymoon at our farm. We had so much fun!! She was used to housekeeping and farm work like it was done in Germany, just as I was, and it sure "threw us" to see how differently things were done over here. One day during their visit I was cooking corn on the cob for supper and Elizabeth came into the kitchen, lifted the lid and had the blankest, most puzzled look on her face. Finally she said, "Oh, you're cooking for the pigs. I thought this was something cooking for supper." I told her it *was* supper (in Germany corn is pig food). We laughed about it and had fun all evening long.

The next year, 1954, passed by and winter arrived. We were still no closer to acquiring electricity but another luxury was added to our little house…a bottle gas stove for the kitchen! I was so glad that I didn't have to haul coal and wood anymore plus having to clean the ashes out of the old stove was dirty and messy. Now I could adjust the burner temperatures and when I turned on the stove there was instant heat. I could hardly believe I had such a wonderful thing!

CHAPTER 27
MY FAMILY ARRIVES IN NORTH DAKOTA

My parents' application papers to come to the United States were being processed faster than we expected. Mama said they could possibly come to the U.S. in early spring already. It seemed like a dream to me that my family would soon be with us in the same country…it had been so long since we were all together in Germany. I missed my homeland so much! I kept in contact with all my uncles, aunts, cousins and friends in Germany. Lotti, my girlfriend, wrote letters to me often. I welcomed this contact, because even with my family nearby in Winnipeg, I was still homesick for Germany and all of our friends and relatives there. Mama said that was because it was where I spent my youth…maybe she was right.

Early in the spring of 1955, Mama, Papa, Herbert and Ellen came to live in the United States. They sold their house in Winnipeg and hired a van to bring their furniture to our farm. We stored it in our barn since our cattle could stay outside now that winter was over. They stayed with us for two weeks. We took them to town often to see if there were jobs available. After a couple of days, Papa went to work for Mayo Construction on street and gutter work in Cavalier. I would take Papa into town in the morning and pick him up at night…it was nine miles from our farm to Cavalier. I was just learning how to drive so I had to stay off the highway. I took the township roads as close to Cavalier as I dared to drive and Papa walked the rest of the way. Mama helped me on the farm. When Papa got his first check, they moved to Cavalier into an apartment on the second floor of a building owned by Kenneth Brandhagen. (Erickson Drug is now located there.) They rented it for $5.00 a week. They hardly took any furnishings with them as they were still looking for a farm job. At this time, I took my driver's test while Mama watched the girls...now I could drive legally.

Mama and Papa continued searching the newspapers for a job on a farm. We would take them around to check them out. They decided to accept work at a farm near Lakota. The couple who owned this farm was old and needed a lot of help. We helped move Mama's and Papa's furniture out there. Mama gave a few pieces of her furniture to me, like the gate-leg table and a couple of plant stands. It was more difficult to get together now as Lakota was almost one hundred miles away from us.

Summer passed by and fall came and Mama and Papa discovered that this wasn't the right job for them. What Papa had hoped to do was take care of milk cows on a dairy farm like he had done in Germany but here he had to do all the farm work and he didn't know how to operate a tractor. He learned a lot, I guess, but not enough so that he could continue working on that farm. At corn harvesting time, Papa didn't know how to fix the machinery when it broke down never mind knowing how to operate it. After the corn was harvested, Mama would go in the fields with baskets and try to pick up all the corn which had fallen off. The farmer thought she was crazy. He said if they did it that way they would never get it finished. It seemed so wasteful to Mama. She said, "I guess I will never make a farmer in this country!"

They quit their job that fall and moved to Grand Forks in hopes of finding better jobs in a bigger city. They found a vacant house on the fairgrounds, asked around, found the owner and were able to rent it. Then they looked for work again. While they were moving into the house and getting settled, Papa kept hearing a lot of noise which he thought sounded like turkeys. There were long barns not too far from the house. One day he walked over there and, with the little English he knew, talked with the man who worked there. He was able to make the man understand that he wanted to work there. By the time he returned home he had a job taking care of the turkeys. Mama found a job, too, cleaning at a mortuary. So within a week, they were able to support themselves again. Herb and Ellen went to a school across from Eddy's Bakery. They liked living there.

As for us on the farm, everything was going along as usual. We were busy getting prepared for winter again. When we helped Mama and Papa move to Grand Forks, I told her we were expecting another baby. Of course, this time it would be a boy since that was what Daddy wanted. I really didn't care. A boy would have been nice, but I had a lot of girls' clothing so it would be cheaper to have a girl.

The winter of 1955 to 1956 came and went. Edith and Karin grew and had lots of fun playing outside in the snow after I bundled them up like little teddy bears. Sometimes Daddy would put them on the stone-boat and our horse, Jim, would pull them all around the yard and the fields. They had a lot of fun in the winter with Daddy and that stone-boat. Later, when Edith and Karin went to the country school, he sometimes took them there on the stone-boat, too.

Spring returned to the farm with all the extra work that comes with it. One day a car came down the road and Mama and Papa were in it. We couldn't believe our eyes!! They had bought an old Ford and Papa had learned to drive. After a few tries, Papa passed his driver's test. They were so proud that they could get around on their own now. Mama said that when the time was near for the baby to be born, they would come and take Edith and Karin back to Grand Forks to stay with them. One weekend in May they came and got them as Mama was so sure I was going to have the baby in the next couple of days. I hated to see my two little girls go. It was the first time we had ever been apart. The girls didn't seem to mind though, as they loved their Grandma and thought it was a treat. It was another whole week before I went to the hospital. Our third little girl, Barbara Noel, was born on May 26, 1956. She had very short, almost fuzzy black hair, blue eyes and weighed eight pounds, one ounce. I was *so* happy to have another daughter. Daddy thought Barbie should have been a boy so he called her "Bob." This time I was in the hospital in Cavalier (it was built two years earlier) so now friends and family could visit.

I got out of the hospital three days later. It happened to be the same day that we were supposed to drive to Grafton to pick up our little baby chicks. So, when we left the hospital, that's what we did! It sure was nice to, finally, get home with our new baby and, of course, all the baby chicks. While the baby was sleeping, we put all the baby chicks in the brooder house.[24] It was a building with a 'brooder' stove[25] in it that warmed it up nicely for the baby chicks. We got them all settled in nicely. The next day we went to get Edith and Karin. They sure loved their new baby sister. They couldn't understand why she had so little hair. We had to re-arrange the house to make room for everything. We put the baby in the crib and Edith and Karin, now five and three years old, slept on the couch, which made into a bed, in the living room. We managed just fine...after all, we had three rooms now!

Spring and summer came with all the usual farm work that's a part of each season. Mama found a new job, as a cook, in the kitchen at St. Michael's Hospital in Grand Forks. She really liked it. She loved to cook and work with food. Papa tried again to find a job taking care of milk cows.

CHAPTER 28

VOICES FROM THE DEAD

One day, in the summer of 1956, I went to the mailbox and found a letter, addressed to me, from Germany. It said the sender was Gerhard Sprung from Lengers, Germany. I thought that it must be a letter for my stepfather, but it had my name on it. And Sprung? Gerhard Sprung? Now, who was that? I went in the house, sat down and read the letter. I just couldn't believe what I was reading. This man was writing about his father! I read that letter about three times before I finally realized what he was saying and what had happened. My heart was overflowing with joy and I felt like leaping into the air. With tears streaming down my face, I looked up to heaven and said, "This is a miracle! Thank you, God!"

The letter had come from Gerhard Sprung, Papa's oldest son. He had learned that his father was still alive and had searched for him for years, but found no trace of him. With help from the Red Cross, Gerhard learned that his father had lived in Klein Zecher. He drove to Klein Zecher and asked folks in that area about him. He was sent to talk to an old friend of ours, Mr. Kaehler. He told Gerhard that his father had married a widow with three children and they had all immigrated to Canada. Mr. Kaehler told Gerhard that he had no idea where they lived but he had the address of their daughter, Ruth, and perhaps Gerhard could write to her and inquire about his father. This, then, was the letter I was reading.

Well...what to do first! The quickest thing I could do was to send the letter on to Grand Forks so they could read the letter themselves. When the letter arrived at their house, Mama read it to Papa. I could only imagine the feelings they must have experienced reading the news. Mama said they were just as puzzled as I was at first, but finally they realized that what they were reading was true. Mama said it was sad to find out that so much time had been lost, but still what a joy!! When Papa heard the news he threw himself on the floor and sobbed like a child. "My son is alive!" he cried, "One of my sons is alive!"

Mama immediately wrote a letter to Gerhard asking lots of questions. It didn't take long before they received an answer back. It turned out that two sons had survived...his two oldest. Gerhard was married and was a butcher in Lengers, Germany. His second son, Emil, was working for a farmer in Germany. In their next letter, Mama and Papa asked if they'd like to come to the United States. They said they would help them by borrowing the money, if necessary, to buy the tickets for their trip. Emil replied that he would like to come but Gerhard was married to an only child, had a home and a good job so would prefer to stay in Germany.

So, once more, there was paperwork to do but, finally, Emil arrived at the Grand Forks airport. What a reunion! Our new brother and Papa's second son! The last time Papa had seen him, Emil was twelve years old... now he was twenty-four. There was so much to say to 'catch up' with all that had happened to them...and what did happen was terrible. Emil told about how they spent the last year of the war. It was a lot worse for them than it was for us. His mother and the six children had gone to Danzig to get on the ship that would take them away...the same one we had heard about. But when they got there and wanted to get on, the boat was so full of people they couldn't have found space even if they'd hung on the outside. After that disappointment, they gave up trying to escape.

They were captured by the Mongolians who were the first troops to come in. His mother was gang raped repeatedly for several days. She and the children got away from the soldiers and decided that they would go back to their hometown. Maybe by some miracle, they would be able to get into their house. After many weeks on the road in the snow and cold with nothing to eat, they made their way back...only to find their house with its windows smashed and, worse, occupied by the enemy. One thing you learn during wartime is that your house is not really your house so they crawled into a shed in the back of the house and tried to survive. At least they were all together. They had found blankets and lots of other items strewn in the streets by the Russians that they could use. That spring, Gerhard and Emil watched their brothers, little five-year old sister and mother starve to death. They all died within the same week. He said he would never forget the sound of his little sister's voice who, as she lay dying, said weakly, "It doesn't hurt anymore." She was the first to die and then his three brothers: seven year old twins and a ten year old. Next their mother died. Gerhard and Emil wrapped the children's bodies in cloths but managed to find some boards to make a box for their mother. They buried all of them in the yard behind the shed.

Gerhard and Emil had some friends who lived some distance away and decided to leave and see if they could find them. They didn't find them and, instead, were used as forced labour for the Russians. Instead of wages the Russians would give them handouts of left-over food from their kitchens, but not regularly. Whatever they would get, they would share with others. There were no stores (and no money) where you could buy any food, only discarded scraps laying in the streets or in abandoned houses. The arrival of summer helped them with their fight for survival.

Gerhard and Emil were now thirteen and fourteen years old and they decided to keep moving westward. They traveled carefully so they would not be captured up by the Russians. If they would have been caught, they would have been sent to Siberia. This happened to so many refugees. When fall and winter arrived, they had made it to East Germany. By working for food and shelter, they managed to survive the winter. When spring came they found a farmer who gave them regular jobs. This was close to the border of West Germany. While working there, they became more and more familiar with their surroundings and when they were a couple of years older, they found the courage to tackle that dangerous stretch of land separating East from West Germany and snuck 'black' across the border.

Once they were across the border, they walked to a small farming village called Lengers, near Bad Hersfeld not realizing that they were already in the west zone. They walked to a farm, knocked on the door and a farm wife answered. They asked for something to eat and asked her if they were in the west. She asked them if they were alone and where they had come from. After they told her where they were from, she invited them in and prepared food for them. She asked them lots of questions and the boys told her their story. She kept them for the night and told them they didn't have to run any more as they were now in the western zone.

In the morning, the farmer told them that one of them (Emil) could stay with them and he'd make arrangements for the other (Gerhard) to help another farmer who had a custom butchering business on his farm. So, Gerhard learned the butchering and sausage making business while Emil learned to be a farm hand. Once they had proven themselves in their respective jobs they received wages for their work. This worked out very well for them and they stayed with these same farmers until Gerhard married and Emil immigrated to the United States.

Emil said that Gerhard still lived in Lengers, Germany but he was glad he immigrated to the United States and he wanted to make it his home. Hearing about Emil and Gerhard's experiences reminded us again of the terrible fear we had, in those days, of being caught by the Red Army and why we made every effort imaginable to escape. People who had been caught by them and had, later, escaped told us about the horrifying things they had endured.

With winter coming again to North Dakota, Papa finally found the job he had been searching for...caring for cows. So they moved, once again, to a farm just north of Grand Forks and worked for the Jensen's. Emil got work on that farm, too. But, after a few months, Emil received a letter from a friend who had immigrated to Cleveland, asking him to come there. So Emil left but before he did, we all spent a wonderful Christmas together on the Jensen farm. Harry and his family came all the way from Sault Ste. Marie, Ontario, where he had been transferred by Crawley Mc-Cracken. His little girl, Irene, was two years old and his little boy, Roland was fifteen months old. Our newest little girl, Barbie, was seven months old. This was a Christmas none of us would ever forget.

CHAPTER 29
BIG CHANGES!

We experienced several changes in the following year of 1957. In the summer my parents decided to leave North Dakota. Mama told me that they tried so hard but just didn't feel at home. Dairy farming was so different here and Papa decided it would be best to give it up. Mama wanted to live where there were lots of German people and German activities. She had heard a lot about Milwaukee, Wisconsin and they decided they'd like to live there. So, in August of 1957 they loaded their belongings in the trunk of that old Ford. What didn't fit in was packed into a giant sized wooden crate and sent by freight train with the address of the Milwaukee train depot on it. It was held there until they picked it up. It hurt me so much to see them go. But what could I do? I wanted what was best for them, too.

They didn't know anyone in Milwaukee, so when they arrived they went to the Salvation Army who helped them until they found an apartment and jobs. Mama and Papa went to the freight station to see if their wooden crate of belongings had arrived. They talked with a guy who worked there and asked him about the crate. He said, "Oh yes, that box created quite a stir, we were all trying to figure out what to do with it." He showed Mama where to go to get the box released to them. Papa's English was still quite poor. The man noticed his German accent, so started speaking German to him. They instantly hit it off and had a good time chatting. Papa told him he needed a job and wondered if the freight depot could use any help. The man said that if he could start the very next day that would be great. Papa was so happy. He worked at the Milwaukee Road Freight Depot for three years. After that he worked as a custodian at a Lutheran church and school until 1970 when he was tragically disabled by a stroke. Mama's references from her job in Grand Forks helped her get work as a cook in a hospital once again. We wrote lots of letters to each other and we went to visit them for the first time, two years later, when Ellen was confirmed.

Another big change that year was our decision to buy a bigger house so we looked around for an older home that could be moved to our property. In March we found a single story, twenty year old house in Bowsemont, twenty-eight miles away. It was a city house, which meant it had plumbing and was wired for electricity. It also had hardwood floors, a 14 by 22 foot living room, three bedrooms, a good-sized dining room and a kitchen. I felt like the best things in life were happening to me! It took most of the summer to dig the basement and get all the arrangements made to move the house. It was quite a journey! Twenty-eight miles! In October we moved into that big house. It didn't even matter that we still did not have plumbing or electricity. I was so happy! The house was ours…we had a room and the girls had a room although Barbie's crib was in our room. The house had so many beautiful windows! We sold our little house to a bachelor and he moved it west of Cavalier (it's still there today). I felt pangs of sadness to see it go. It held memories from a big part of my life, but at the same time it was easy to let it go.

Barbie was one year old when we moved into the big house. She was such a fun little child. Karin was four now and Edith was six. In the fall, Edith started school at Ormely Country school about 2¼ miles away. We were getting all settled into our new home now and Karin was such a good little helper.

The year 1958 began with much sadness. In January of that year Uncle Alex came over to tell us that Ruby, Daddy's sister, had passed away suddenly. This was such a shock and we were all devastated. She was only thirty-five years old and had died of a heart problem. Catherine and David were only thirteen and eleven years old and it was so difficult for them. Grandma Peil helped Alex raise them.

Wonderful changes awaited us later that year…big wonderful changes! Without electricity our new house seemed so dark in the evenings… especially because it was so big. At night we had to carry the lamp with us into every room. Finally, we were able to get electricity and it was so amazing! Since the house was already wired, all they had to do was hook it up. There were no more long shadows at night and every room was so bright. That first evening I turned on the lights in every room and just looked…drinking it all in. It was too good to be true. Besides the lights it was, also, wonderful to have an electric washing machine and, eventually a refrigerator.

In the winter of 1958-1959, Papa flew to Germany to see his eldest son, Gerhard. Gerhard was thirteen years old the last time Papa had seen him. The reunion was filled with joy. By this time, Emil had married a German girl in Cleveland and had moved to Milwaukee. Papa was happy and content to have at least one member of his family nearby.

Ellen came to our farm and stayed with us every summer for four to six weeks. Do you girls remember that? All four of you played and did a lot of things together…some good, some not so good. Of course, the not-so-good things I found out about much later! Herb, also, came periodically and stayed. I was so glad you grew up together and got to know each other so well. It is so important for families to be close.

From this point on, girls, I think you can remember our life on the farm. I hope you will pick up a pen and write down your memories to share with your children and their children. I pray that you all, now married, will stay close to one another and help and support each other. My mama passed her faith on to me and now I see that the God who lives in my heart also lives in my daughters' and grandchildren's hearts…a legacy from my mother…and, so, I thank you, my precious Mama. I say to you, all three of my daughters, *Bete und Arbeit,* and God will show you the way!

With love to each of you,

Mama

Our family in January of 2006. From left to right behind Mama is Ruth, Herbert, Harry, and Ellen.

MY FAMILY...WHERE ARE THEY NOW?

Papa, Emil Sprung:

Papa loved to fish and spent as many spare hours as he could fishing and, often, took his children and grandchildren along with him to share in the fun. Papa continued to work as a custodian at the Lutheran Church and School until he suffered a severe stroke in 1970 which left him partially paralyzed. Mama cared for him at home until his health deteriorated further and he required special care in a nursing home. He lived in the nursing home in Milwaukee for almost eleven years and then was moved to a care centre in Williams Bay, Wisconsin, where he lived a few more months before he passed away in 1983.

Mama, Ida Preuss Garn Sprung:

Mama continued to work at the hospital until she retired. After Papa was hospitalized, she sold their home to pay for the hospital bills. She rented an apartment until 1993 and, then, lived with Ellen. Beginning in 1998 she shared her time between Ellen's home and mine. Mama stayed with her for several months and then with me for several months...over the years we did the 500 mile journey between our homes many times. By the latter part of 2007 it was becoming obvious that Mama required more care than we were able to give and in January 2008, Mama signed her own papers to admit herself into a nursing home. She is still residing there today and likes it very much. Mama will celebrate her 100th birthday on October 1st and is looking forward to receiving a birthday card from the president!

My brother, Harry Garn:

Harry and his wife, Elizabeth, have lived in Empire, Michigan since 1971. They had three children, Irene, Roland and Kristie and have one grand-daughter. In January of 1968, when Irene was thirteen years old, she was hit by a car and died. My dear brother and his family suffered the loss of their beloved daughter and sister and we all mourned with them. Harry continued to work in food service for various companies until he suffered a massive stroke in 2006. The stroke was devastating and left him paralyzed on his right side and unable to speak. He is now living in a nursing home and is confined to a wheelchair. Harry and I had always talked a lot about our experiences in Germany and the war…he was the *only* one I could talk about those times with who truly understood because he went through them with me and now we cannot share our memories anymore…I so mourn that loss.

My brother, Herbert Garn:

My brother, Herbert worked for the U.S. Forest Service and Geological Survey until he retired, as a hydrologist, in 2008. He and his wife, Fran, live in Madison, Wisconsin and have three children, John, Carrie and Nathan. They have four grandchildren at this time.

My sister, Ellen Sprung Weber:

Ellen and her husband, David, live on an acreage near Williams Bay, Wisconsin. She does a lot of philanthropic work on behalf of the developmentally disabled as well as other local charities and civic groups. They raised seven children; Kurt, Spencer, Chris, Sara, Stacey, David and Derek. They have nine grandchildren.

Ruth Garn Werner:

In 1965 we gave up farming and moved to Sioux Falls, South Dakota...my brother, Harry and his family were living there at the time. It was so difficult to leave the farm where I felt secure because of the dependable food supply but I, also, knew in my heart that this was God's will and the right thing to do. I had a hard life on the farm, not to mention I had suffered a serious farming accident two years earlier which left me with lifelong injuries that made it difficult for me to walk. So, God was watching out for me again and led me to an easier life. Immediately after we moved to Sioux Falls, Helmut

Ruth Garn Werner

found a job at a service station and I worked at a nursing home. It wasn't too long before we got better jobs, Helmut worked as a custodian and I got a job at Raven Industries. There, I worked my way up from assembly line sewer to production coordinator/trouble shooter. I loved working at Raven's! Helmut and I were divorced in 1980 but we still maintained lots of family contact until he passed away after an accident in 1986. My three daughters have all married and have children and grandchildren of their own. After thirty-three years I retired and I live in the same house we bought after moving to Sioux Falls. These thirteen years of retirement have been the best years of my life. Besides caring for my Mama I have been busy with many other activities as well. I am an avid gardener...both flower and vegetable. I am very busy at my church singing in the choir, quilting, attending women's Bible studies, working in Senior Ministry and volunteering whenever and wherever I am able. I always look forward to the many visits I receive from my ten grandchildren and I consider it a privilege that I am able to babysit frequently for my great-grandchildren... seventeen of them so far! I live alone, but I am never really alone...my Lord and Saviour are with me every step of the way. My faith, my children and my grandchildren are my life...and when I see that they have the Lord in their life, I am ever so thankful...Amen.

ENDNOTES

[1] Similar to a county or municipal district in U.S. or Canada, often abbreviated as Kr.

[2] Where both sides in a military confrontation or war meet…the most intensive fighting

[3] Kilometre (1 kilometre = 0.6 mile)

[4] Our sleigh had runners with a bench seat that could hold three people

[5] A sports field

[6] Kilogram (1 kilogram=2.2 pounds)

[7] Often called the poor man's coffee…made from the roasted and ground roots of the chicory plant

[8] A guest house

[9] Grandmother

[10] Mr.

[11] Grandfather

[12] Celsius (-20C = -6F) (-30C = -22F)

[13] From the hymn 'Lord, Take My Hand and Lead me', Text written by Julie von Hausmann (1825-1901).

[14] Reichsmark…the German currency from 1924 until June 1948 when it was replaced by the Deutsche Mark

[15] Aunt

[16] Uncle

[17] Metre (one metre = 39.4 inches)

[18] Viral hepatitis

[19] A small wagon made for Panja horses, a small, strong Russian breed

[20] A variety of beets raised for feed for livestock

[21] From Greek word 'light bearing.' At one time was present in engine/lube oil and emits a glow when exposed to oxygen

[22] Used to provide drinking water for animals such as cattle or horses. Stock tanks can range in size from 30 to over 1500 gallons and are usually made of galvanized steel

[23] A device for moving heavy objects such as stones or hay bales. It was used with horses by the settlers of the American West, and is still sometimes used with tractors today

[24] A heated building for chicks

[25] A stove used to heat a brooder house, often with a metal umbrella type cover on it that chicks could gather under for extra warmth